the pawnee native american tribe for kids

Journey into Pawnee Culture

sarah michaels

Copyright © 2024 by Sarah Michaels

All rights reserved.

No part of this book may be reproduced in any form or by any electronic or mechanical means, including information storage and retrieval systems, without written permission from the author, except for the use of brief quotations in a book review.

1 / who are the pawnee?

LONG BEFORE THE first train chugged across the plains or any roads were paved, the Pawnee lived in villages near rivers. These rivers, like the Platte and Loup Rivers in Nebraska, provided the water they needed to grow crops, drink, and cook food. Water was also important because it allowed the Pawnee to stay connected to nature, which was a huge part of their world. Nature was more than just something around them—it was part of their lives in a very special way. The sun, the moon, and the stars played a big role in how they lived and the things they believed in.

For the Pawnee, the sky was like a giant calendar. They looked to the stars to know when to plant their crops and when to prepare for the hunting seasons. When they gazed at the night sky, they didn't just see twinkling lights. They saw stories, guides, and even their ancestors watching over them. Some of these stars had names, and the Pawnee believed they were connected to different spirits. These spirits were important because they helped explain the world around them. It was almost like how people today look at weather reports to plan their days, but for the Pawnee, looking up at the stars told them what they needed to do to live their lives.

One of the most important crops the Pawnee grew was corn. They had a deep connection to corn, and it wasn't just food for them—it was part of their spiritual world. They believed corn was a gift from the Creator, and they treated it with great respect. Pawnee women were responsible for planting and tending the corn, and they used clever farming methods to make sure the crops would grow strong. They didn't have tractors or modern tools, but they knew how to use the land in ways that kept it healthy year after year. In the spring, the Pawnee would hold special ceremonies to make sure the crops would grow, and they celebrated when the corn was ready to be harvested.

While the women took care of the crops, the men were often out hunting. The Pawnee were excellent hunters, and their favorite animal to hunt was the buffalo. Buffalo weren't just a source of meat for the Pawnee—they provided everything from clothing to tools. When a Pawnee hunter brought down a buffalo, every part of the animal was used. The hide became blankets or clothing, the bones turned into tools, and even the horns could be made into cups. Nothing went to waste.

To hunt buffalo, the Pawnee had to be smart and brave. Imagine standing in front of a huge, thundering herd of buffalo, each one bigger than a car! The Pawnee developed a special way of hunting them by working together. Sometimes, they would lead the buffalo toward cliffs or trap them in a way that made hunting them easier. The Pawnee also relied on fast horses to chase down the buffalo during hunts, and their skill with bows and arrows meant they rarely missed their target.

Horses were another important part of the Pawnee's lives. But did you know that horses weren't always a part of Native American culture? The Spanish explorers brought horses to North America, and the Pawnee, along with other tribes, quickly learned how to ride and care for these powerful animals. Horses changed the way the Pawnee hunted and traveled, allowing them to move more quickly and cover greater distances. With horses, they could hunt more buffalo and travel farther across the plains.

Although buffalo hunting was a big part of their lives, the Pawnee couldn't rely on hunting alone. That's why they lived in villages for most of the year, where they could farm and build homes. Their homes, called earth lodges, were incredible structures. They were built mostly by women and were made from a wooden frame covered with dirt and grass. This made them cool in the summer and warm in the winter, perfect for the ever-changing weather on the Great Plains. Earth lodges were usually round, with a hole in the center of the roof to let smoke from the fire escape. Inside, families slept on raised platforms, and everyone gathered around the fire for warmth and cooking.

Life inside a Pawnee village was busy but balanced. There was always something to do—whether it was tending crops, repairing homes, or preparing food—but the Pawnee also knew how to relax and enjoy themselves. Storytelling was a huge part of their culture, and after a long day of work, they would gather around the fire to listen to tales of their ancestors, their gods, and their heroes. These stories weren't just for fun; they passed down important lessons and traditions from one generation to the next. The Pawnee believed that these stories connected them to their past and helped them understand the world around them.

One of the most important parts of Pawnee life was their belief in gods and spirits. They believed that everything around them—the sun, the stars, the wind, the animals—had its own spirit. They honored these spirits with ceremonies and songs, asking for their guidance and protection. One of the biggest celebrations was the Morning Star Ceremony, where the Pawnee honored the Morning Star, which they believed was a powerful god.

These ceremonies were full of singing, dancing, and prayer, and they helped the Pawnee feel connected to the world around them.

where they lived

The Great Plains stretched out like a giant ocean of grass. If you stood in the middle of it, you could look in every direction and not see a single mountain or tall tree—just endless stretches of land. This is where the Pawnee lived, right in the heart of the Great Plains. It was a land that might seem empty or quiet to someone passing through, but to the Pawnee, it was home. Every part of the Plains had something to offer, and the Pawnee knew how to live in harmony with this vast landscape.

The Great Plains are a huge area of flat, grassy land that spreads across the central part of North America, from what we now call Texas all the way up into Canada. The wind is a constant companion, sweeping across the land, sometimes gently, sometimes with great force. It's a place where the seasons change dramatically—freezing cold winters and blistering hot summers—but the Pawnee had learned how to thrive in this challenging environment. For them, the Great Plains weren't just a piece of land. They were the center of their lives, their culture, and their connection to the natural world.

One of the most important features of the Great Plains

was the rivers. The Pawnee built their villages near rivers like the Platte, Loup, and Republican because these waterways were essential to their way of life. The rivers provided fresh water for drinking, cooking, and farming, but they also served as highways, connecting different Pawnee villages and allowing them to travel and trade with other tribes. The rivers would swell with life in the spring, and along their banks, plants and animals would flourish. The Pawnee didn't just live by the rivers—they depended on them, and the rhythm of the water shaped the rhythm of their lives.

If you were to walk through a Pawnee village, you'd notice how close it was to the earth. Their homes, called earth lodges, were built from the very ground they lived on. These homes were perfectly suited for life on the Plains. The thick walls made from packed earth and grass kept the lodges warm in the winter and cool in the summer. Inside, families would gather around a central fire, and everything from daily meals to important ceremonies happened under the roof of the earth lodge. The Plains might seem like a harsh place to live, but the Pawnee had figured out how to make it work, building homes that blended right into the landscape.

The land around them wasn't empty—it was filled with life. Herds of buffalo roamed the Plains, moving across the grasslands like dark clouds. These animals were vital to the Pawnee's survival. A single buffalo could provide food, clothing, and tools, and the Pawnee had developed special techniques for hunting these giant creatures. The buffalo was more than just a source of meat; it was central to their culture. They used almost every part of the buffalo, from the bones to the hide, and they honored the animal in ceremonies and stories. The buffalo was a symbol of life on the Plains, representing the connection between the Pawnee and the natural world.

The Plains were also home to other animals, like deer, antelope, and wolves, and each one played a role in the Pawnee's understanding of the world. The wolves, for example, were respected for their hunting skills and their ability to survive in the harshest conditions. The Pawnee often told stories about wolves and saw them as protectors of the tribe. The land and the animals weren't separate from the Pawnee—they were all connected. The Plains weren't just a place to live; they were alive with stories, lessons, and meaning.

The wide-open spaces of the Great Plains also meant that the sky played a big role in the lives of the Pawnee. Without tall buildings or mountains in the way, the sky stretched endlessly above them, and at night, it was filled with stars. The Pawnee believed that the stars were more than just lights in the sky. To them, the stars were a guide, helping them navigate the seasons and their lives. They looked up at constellations like the Morning Star and the Evening Star, which were important symbols in their spiritual beliefs. These stars weren't just faraway objects—they were part of the Pawnee's world, helping them understand when to plant crops, when to hunt, and how to stay connected to the universe.

But life on the Plains wasn't always easy. The weather could be unpredictable, with fierce storms sweeping across the land, bringing heavy rain or even hail. The Pawnee knew how to prepare for these challenges. They paid close attention to the signs in nature, like the way the wind shifted or how the clouds moved, to predict changes in the weather. They didn't have weather reports or technology like we do today, but their understanding of the land and the sky helped them survive.

One of the things that made the Pawnee special was their deep connection to the land. They didn't see the land as something to be taken or controlled. Instead, they saw themselves as part of it. The earth, the sky, the rivers, and the animals were all connected, and the Pawnee lived their lives in harmony with this understanding. This connection to the land was something they passed down through generations, teaching their children to respect the world around them and to see the beauty and importance of the Plains.

The Great Plains were also a place where the Pawnee would meet other tribes. The Plains weren't just home to the Pawnee—they shared the land with many other Native American tribes, like the Sioux and the Cheyenne. Sometimes these tribes would trade with each other, sharing goods like food, tools, and horses. Other times, they would fight to protect their land and resources. The Plains were a vast space, but they were also a place of interaction and connection between different cultures.

brief overview of their history and culture

The Pawnee are believed to have lived on the Plains for over a thousand years. They settled in what is now Nebraska and Kansas, where they established villages made up of earth lodges, those round homes with thick, sturdy walls built from the earth itself. The way they farmed and lived in these villages set them apart from many other tribes. While others relied mainly on hunting and gathering, the Pawnee were expert farmers. They grew crops like corn, beans, and squash, which helped them survive in times when hunting wasn't as fruitful. Corn, especially, was central to their life and their beliefs.

The Pawnee didn't just farm and hunt, though. They had a rich spiritual life that shaped their everyday actions. Imagine looking up at the stars every night, not just because they were pretty, but because they guided you. The Pawnee were known for their incredible knowledge of the stars. They believed that the stars told them when to plant their crops and when to hunt. The stars weren't just distant lights to them—they were part of their spiritual world, each one connected to a spirit or god. One of the most important stars was the Morning Star, which played a big role in their religious ceremonies. The Morning Star was believed to bring new life and protect the people, and the Pawnee celebrated its rise in special ceremonies filled with prayers, songs, and dances.

The Pawnee divided themselves into different bands or groups, each with its own identity, but they all shared a common language and many of the same traditions. These bands would sometimes live close to one another, and other times they would spread out across the Plains, depending on the needs of the season. The four main bands were the Skidi, the Chaui, the Kitkahahki, and the Pitahawirata. Each band had its own leaders and special ceremonies, but they all came together for major events and to make important decisions for the tribe as a whole.

One of the most important aspects of Pawnee culture was their connection to the earth and sky. Their spiritual beliefs weren't just about worshipping distant gods—they saw the entire world around them as alive and filled with spirits. The earth, the rivers, the wind, and the animals all had spirits that could guide and protect them. When they hunted buffalo or planted corn, it wasn't just a task to get food—it was part of a bigger relationship with the world around them. Every action was filled with meaning, and they believed that showing respect to the land and animals would ensure that they continued to be blessed with what they needed to survive.

Because of this close relationship with nature, the Pawnee held many ceremonies throughout the year. These ceremonies were not only a way to ask for blessings or give thanks but also a way to bring the community together. During these ceremonies, Pawnee men and women would dress in special clothing, often decorated with feathers, beads, and paint, to show their connection to the spiritual world. They would dance, sing, and tell stories that had been passed down through generations. These stories were more than just entertainment—they were a way to remember their history and keep their culture alive. Through these ceremonies, the Pawnee honored their gods and ancestors, asking for their protection and guidance.

Warriors were highly respected in Pawnee culture. The men of the tribe were responsible for protecting their people and their land, and they took this role very seriously. Warriors would often go on raids against other tribes, both to defend their territory and to show their bravery. Being a warrior wasn't just about fighting, though. It was about courage, honor, and doing what was right for the community. A warrior's success wasn't measured only by how many battles they won, but by how they conducted themselves in those battles—how they respected their enemies and protected their own people.

But the Pawnee weren't always at war. Much of their time was spent working together in peace to farm, hunt, and take care of their villages. Pawnee society valued cooperation, and everyone had a role to play. Women were responsible for farming, cooking, and maintaining the earth lodges, while men hunted and defended the tribe. Children were taught from a young age to contribute to the community, learning important skills from their parents and elders. Pawnee children were raised with a deep understanding of their culture and the importance of working together.

As time went on, the Pawnee's world began to change. When European settlers arrived in North America, they brought new ideas, animals, and technologies—but they also brought conflict. The settlers wanted the same land that the Pawnee had lived on for generations. This created tension, and eventually, the Pawnee were forced to fight to protect their land and way of life. As more settlers came westward, the buffalo herds began to disappear, making it harder for the Pawnee to survive. The loss of buffalo, combined with diseases brought by the Europeans, created enormous challenges for the tribe.

The U.S. government also played a role in changing the lives of the Pawnee. As settlers moved west, the government began pushing Native American tribes off their land and onto reservations. The Pawnee, like many other tribes, were forced to leave their homes and relocate to reservations in what is now Oklahoma. This was a difficult time for the Pawnee, as they were no longer able to live as they once had. They could no longer hunt buffalo freely, and their way of farming had to change to fit the new environment. Despite these challenges, the Pawnee held onto their culture and traditions, passing down their stories, ceremonies, and beliefs to future generations.

2 / the pawnee way of life

the pawnee villages and homes

PAWNEE VILLAGES WERE USUALLY LOCATED near rivers, where the land was fertile and water was plentiful. The rivers didn't just supply water for drinking and farming—they also provided clay, grass, and wood, which the Pawnee used to build their earth lodges. These villages were carefully planned, with the earth lodges arranged in a circular pattern around a central open space, where ceremonies, games, and gatherings took place. The layout of the village showed the Pawnee's sense of community. Everyone lived close to one another, and the central space was where the entire village could come together, whether it was to celebrate a harvest or hold a spiritual ceremony.

Building an earth lodge was a community effort. It

started with a strong frame made from logs, usually cottonwood or willow trees that grew along the riverbanks. These logs were placed in a circular pattern, leaning inward to create a dome shape. Once the frame was complete, the Pawnee covered it with thick layers of packed earth and grass. This natural insulation made the lodges incredibly sturdy, keeping them cool during the scorching summers and warm during the freezing winters. In fact, earth lodges were so well-built that they could last for many years, sometimes even decades, with only a little bit of maintenance.

Inside the earth lodge, life centered around the hearth, or fire pit, which sat in the middle of the room. The smoke from the fire would rise up through a hole in the roof, keeping the lodge warm and providing a place to cook food. The fire wasn't just for warmth or cooking, though—it also had a spiritual meaning for the Pawnee. The hearth was a symbol of the home's connection to the earth, and it was always treated with respect. Around the hearth, Pawnee families gathered to eat, tell stories, and share their day.

The inside of the lodge was cleverly designed to make the most of the space. Raised platforms, made from wooden poles and covered with animal hides, lined the walls. These platforms served as both beds and seating areas during the day. The walls were often decorated with beautifully crafted items like woven baskets, pottery, and tools. Every corner of the lodge had a purpose, whether it was for storing food, hanging up tools, or preparing meals. There was little waste of space, and everything had its place.

While the earth lodge might seem simple on the outside, it was filled with meaning. The circular shape wasn't just practical—it represented the Pawnee's view of the world. They believed that life was a continuous cycle, much like the seasons or the movement of the stars. The lodge, with its round design, reflected this belief. It symbolized the connection between the people, the earth, and the sky. Living in a circle meant living in balance, and the Pawnee believed that everything in life was connected—family, nature, and the spirits.

Because the lodges were built from natural materials, they blended right into the landscape. From a distance, it might have been hard to even spot a Pawnee village. The domed roofs, covered in grass, looked like small hills rising from the earth. This connection to the land wasn't just physical—it was spiritual as well. The Pawnee believed that the earth was alive and sacred, and by building their homes from the earth itself, they honored that belief.

During the summer months, the village was a busy place. Pawnee women were hard at work tending the fields of corn, beans, and squash, while the men prepared for buffalo hunts. Children would run and play in the open spaces between the lodges, learning the skills they would need as adults. The central area of the village was often filled with activity—ceremonies, dances, or meetings where important decisions were made. The village wasn't just a place to live—it was the heart of Pawnee life, where everyone worked together to ensure the survival and success of the community.

When winter arrived, life in the village changed. The cold winds swept across the Plains, but the thick walls of the earth lodges kept the families warm. Inside the lodges, life slowed down. Families gathered around the fire, telling stories and passing down traditions to the younger generation. The winter months were a time for rest and reflection, but also a time to prepare for the year ahead. The stories told during these long winter nights weren't just for entertainment—they were a way to teach lessons, share history, and keep the culture alive.

The earth lodge was more than just a house—it was a home that connected the Pawnee people to each other and to the land around them. It was a place where families could gather, where children learned about their culture, and where traditions were passed down from one generation to the next. The lodges, with their thick walls and sturdy roofs, represented the strength and resilience of the

Pawnee people, who had lived on the Great Plains for centuries.

daily life

At the heart of Pawnee life was farming. The Pawnee were expert farmers, and their main crop was corn, which they called "maize." But they didn't just grow corn—they also planted beans, squash, and sunflowers. Together, these crops made sure the Pawnee had enough food to eat, even when the hunting wasn't as good. Farming wasn't just a job for the Pawnee; it was a tradition passed down through generations. The knowledge of when to plant, how to tend the crops, and when to harvest was something that every Pawnee family took pride in.

In the spring, Pawnee women would begin preparing the fields for planting. Using wooden tools, they would dig into the earth and carefully place each seed into the ground. The women were in charge of farming, and they had a special connection to the crops they grew. Corn, especially, was more than just food—it was part of the Pawnee's spiritual life. They believed that the corn had been given to them by the Creator, and they held ceremonies to ensure a good harvest. These ceremonies were a way of thanking the earth for its gifts and asking for its continued blessings.

As the crops grew taller, the women and children would spend time in the fields, weeding and making sure that everything was growing strong. The sun was hot, and the work was hard, but there was also joy in seeing the crops grow and knowing that they would provide food for the entire village. Farming required patience and care, and it was something that brought the Pawnee people together. Families often worked side by side in the fields, sharing stories and songs as they worked.

While the women tended to the crops, the men focused on hunting. Hunting was a vital part of Pawnee life, and buffalo were the most important animals they hunted. The buffalo provided meat for food, hides for clothing and shelter, and bones for tools. The entire buffalo was used, and nothing was wasted. Buffalo hunting was dangerous and required skill, courage, and teamwork. Pawnee hunters would travel far from their villages, often on horseback, to follow the herds. They would wait for the right moment to strike, using bows and arrows to bring down the animals.

Hunting wasn't just about providing food—it was also a way for the men to show their bravery and skill. Young boys would watch and learn from their fathers and uncles, practicing their aim with small bows and arrows and dreaming of the day they could join the hunt. Hunting was a way to protect and provide for the family, and it was one of the most important responsibilities a Pawnee man could have.

But buffalo weren't the only animals the Pawnee hunted. They also hunted deer, rabbits, and other animals that roamed the Great Plains. Each hunt required careful planning and strategy, and every animal was respected. The Pawnee believed that the animals they hunted had spirits, and they gave thanks to those spirits after a successful hunt. This respect for nature was a big part of Pawnee life. The Pawnee never took more than they needed, and they made sure to use every part of the animal, from the meat to the bones.

While farming and hunting were the two main activities in the village, family life was just as important. Everyone in the village had a role to play, from the youngest children to the elders. Families were at the center of Pawnee life, and they worked together to make sure everyone was taken care of. Children were taught to respect their elders and to listen to their stories. These stories weren't just for fun—they were a way to pass down history and traditions. Through these stories, children learned about their ancestors, the spirits, and the world around them.

The elders in the village held a special place in Pawnee society. They were the keepers of knowledge and the ones who guided the younger generations. They didn't work in the fields or go on hunts anymore, but they were still active in the village. Elders would often be found sitting around the fire, sharing their wisdom with anyone who would listen. Their advice was valuable, and their stories reminded everyone of the importance of community and tradition.

Children in Pawnee villages were given important tasks from a young age. They would help their mothers in the fields, learn how to gather wood for the fires, and practice hunting skills with their fathers. Boys and girls had different roles to prepare them for adulthood. Boys would learn to hunt, make tools, and protect the village, while girls would learn how to farm, cook, and take care of the home. These skills were taught with patience and care, and children were encouraged to do their best. There was no rush, but every day brought new lessons and new responsibilities.

As children grew older, they took on more responsibilities within the family and the village. Teenagers would often join in hunting trips or take on bigger roles in the fields. Young women would begin learning the more complex tasks of running a household, while young men would start training as warriors, learning to defend their village and their people. By the time a Pawnee child became an adult, they were well-prepared for the roles they would play in the community.

The Pawnee also placed a great deal of importance on community celebrations and ceremonies. These events were a time to come together, not just as individual families but as a whole village. Ceremonies often revolved around the cycles of the seasons, especially the planting and harvest times. During these celebrations, everyone had a role to play. Women would prepare large meals, the men might perform ritual dances, and children would watch in awe as the elders shared stories of the past. The entire village would sing and dance, giving thanks to the earth and the spirits for providing for them.

importance of community and cooperation

Life in a Pawnee village was built on the idea that everyone was part of a larger whole. From farming to hunting, from storytelling to ceremonies, everything that the Pawnee did was tied to the community. No one lived for themselves alone. Whether young or old, each person had a role that helped the entire village thrive. For the Pawnee, cooperation wasn't just something that happened when it was convenient—it was at the heart of how they survived and lived together on the Great Plains.

The sense of community started with the family. Pawnee families lived together in the earth lodges, and everyone had responsibilities. Mothers and fathers worked to make sure their children had food, shelter, and clothing, but they also taught them how to be part of the larger group. In the mornings, families would often share a meal together before going about their tasks. A mother might take her daughters to the fields to show them how to care for the crops, while a father might teach his sons the skills of hunting or tool-making. But these lessons weren't just about how to plant or hunt—they were about how to work with others, to listen, and to help when needed.

In Pawnee culture, cooperation was essential for survival. The work of growing food, building homes, and hunting animals required many hands. One person couldn't do it all alone, and the Pawnee knew that. When the time came to plant the fields, women from different families would work together. They'd gather in groups, chatting and sharing stories as they carefully placed the seeds into the ground. The work was hard, but when done together, it became a social event as much as a task. The same went for harvest time, when everyone came together to gather the crops that would feed the village through the winter.

The men, too, relied on teamwork. Hunting buffalo wasn't something a single person could do by themselves. Buffalo were massive animals, and bringing one down required careful planning and cooperation. Hunters would often travel in groups, coordinating their efforts to corner the buffalo and bring it down. Each hunter had a role to play, and the success of the hunt depended on everyone doing their part. If one person decided to act on their own, it could put the entire group in danger. Trust and cooperation were the keys to a successful hunt, and the Pawnee understood that working together wasn't just practical—it was necessary.

But cooperation didn't stop with farming and hunting. It extended to every part of Pawnee life. Ceremonies and celebrations, which were such an important part of the Pawnee culture, also relied on the whole community coming together. Whether it was a ceremony to honor the spirits or a celebration of the harvest, everyone had a role to play. Some people might be in charge of preparing food, while others led dances or played music. The elders often took on the role of storytellers, passing down the legends and history of the Pawnee people. During these events, the entire village gathered as one, sharing in the joy, the prayers, and the sense of unity that came from being part of something larger than themselves.

Children learned about cooperation from an early age. They were taught that their actions affected not just themselves, but everyone around them. If a child helped in the fields or learned to sew a warm blanket, they weren't just doing a chore—they were contributing to the well-being of the village. The Pawnee believed that by teaching children to cooperate, they were ensuring the future strength of the community. As children grew older, their responsibilities grew too, but they were never alone in learning. Older siblings, parents, and even the elders in the village all helped guide them, showing them the value of working together.

Even in times of hardship, the Pawnee relied on their sense of community. When the weather turned harsh, when crops didn't grow as expected, or when a hunting trip wasn't successful, the village pulled together. Families would share food, help repair damaged homes, and make sure that no one was left to struggle on their own. This sense of responsibility for one another was a cornerstone of Pawnee life. The idea was that by helping others, you were also helping yourself, because a strong community meant a strong future for everyone.

One of the clearest examples of cooperation among the Pawnee was seen during their large communal hunts or when they built new earth lodges. Constructing an earth lodge wasn't something a single family could do alone. It required a group effort, with people gathering wood for the frame, others packing the earth to form the walls, and still others weaving grass and branches to create the roof. These building projects would bring the entire village together, with people contributing their strengths and skills. When the work was finished, there would often be a celebration, not just to mark the completion of the lodge, but to honor the cooperation that made it possible.

Even the way the Pawnee made decisions showed their focus on cooperation. Important matters, like decisions about where to hunt or how to protect the village, were discussed by the leaders of the community. These leaders, often elders or respected warriors, would gather to talk, debate, and eventually agree on a course of action. They didn't just make decisions on their own—they listened to the needs and opinions of others in the village. The goal was always to come to a decision that was best for the whole community, not just for a few individuals.

3 /
the pawnee and the buffalo

OUT ON THE GREAT PLAINS, the buffalo were everywhere. Huge, shaggy creatures that roamed in herds so large they seemed to stretch out forever. For the Pawnee, these animals were more than just something they saw in the distance. Buffalo were a vital part of their lives. They weren't just animals to hunt—they were essential for survival. Almost every part of the buffalo was used by the Pawnee, and because of this, they treated the buffalo with great respect.

The relationship between the Pawnee and the buffalo was one of balance and gratitude. The buffalo provided food, shelter, tools, and clothing, and in return, the Pawnee showed respect for the buffalo's spirit. They believed that if they hunted the buffalo with care and gratitude, the animals would continue to provide for them. This wasn't just a practical relationship; it was also deeply spiritual.

The Pawnee honored the buffalo with ceremonies and prayers, thanking them for their sacrifices.

The most obvious way the Pawnee relied on the buffalo was for food. The meat from a single buffalo could feed many people, and because the herds were so large, the Pawnee could hunt enough buffalo to provide for their entire village. When the hunters brought a buffalo back to the village, the women would begin the careful process of butchering the animal. Nothing was wasted. The meat was divided up, with some being eaten right away and the rest being preserved for later. The Pawnee had a clever way of drying the meat, turning it into jerky that could last through the long winter months when hunting wasn't always possible.

But the buffalo wasn't just food for the Pawnee. The hides, or skins, of the buffalo were incredibly useful. After the meat was removed, the hides were stretched out and tanned, a process that made them soft and durable. These buffalo hides were then used to make clothing, blankets, and coverings for their homes. The thick hide kept out the cold during the freezing winters, and Pawnee families would wrap themselves in buffalo blankets to stay warm.

The hides were also used to make moccasins, the shoes that Pawnee people wore to protect their feet as they walked across the rough terrain of the Plains. The moccasins were sturdy but soft, allowing the Pawnee to move quietly while hunting or traveling. When you wore moccasins, you could feel connected to the earth beneath your feet, which was something the Pawnee valued deeply.

Even the buffalo's bones were put to use. The bones were carved into tools and weapons, such as knives, scrapers, and arrowheads. They were strong and durable, making them perfect for cutting, shaping, and building. The horns of the buffalo were also useful—they could be hollowed out and used as containers or turned into cups and spoons. Imagine drinking water from a buffalo horn or using a buffalo bone knife to prepare food! The Pawnee were skilled at making sure nothing from the buffalo went to waste.

Buffalo sinew, which is a tough, fibrous tissue, was another valuable resource. The Pawnee used sinew to make strong thread, which was perfect for sewing clothing and stitching together other items made from buffalo hide. They also used sinew to make bowstrings, which had to be both flexible and strong in order to be effective during a hunt. With every part of the buffalo being used, the Pawnee didn't need much else in terms of materials. The buffalo truly provided for nearly all their needs.

While the meat, hides, and bones were the most commonly used parts of the buffalo, there were even more ways the Pawnee relied on these animals. The buffalo's fat was rendered into tallow, which could be used to make soap or candles. The stomach lining was sometimes used as a container to hold water or other liquids. The tail of the buffalo could be fashioned into a fly swatter, and even the hooves were melted down to create glue. It's incredible to think about how every single part of the buffalo could be turned into something useful.

Hunting buffalo was an essential skill for the Pawnee men, and it was something they took seriously. The hunt itself was a well-planned event, requiring cooperation, strategy, and bravery. The men would often go out in groups, sometimes on foot and other times on horseback, to follow the herds. Hunting on horseback gave the Pawnee a great advantage. Their horses were fast and agile, allowing them to get close to the buffalo without spooking the herd. The Pawnee hunters were skilled with bows and arrows, able to take down a buffalo with precision.

Buffalo hunting wasn't just about skill, though—it was also dangerous. A buffalo was a massive animal, often weighing over a thousand pounds, and if it charged, it could be deadly. That's why the Pawnee worked together to make the hunt as safe and efficient as possible. They relied on their knowledge of the land and the behavior of the buffalo to help them. Sometimes, they would drive a herd toward a natural barrier, like a cliff or a river, making it easier to trap and kill the animals without putting themselves in too much danger.

Once the buffalo was brought back to the village, the

entire community came together to process the animal. The women played a vital role in preparing the buffalo, while the men took pride in knowing that they had provided for their families. The successful hunt was often followed by a ceremony or celebration, where the Pawnee would thank the spirits for their good fortune and give thanks to the buffalo for providing so much.

The spiritual connection between the Pawnee and the buffalo was woven into every aspect of their lives. They believed that the buffalo was a gift from the Creator, and that by respecting the animal, they were honoring the Creator's gift. This belief shaped the way the Pawnee hunted, used, and thought about the buffalo. Even when they needed the buffalo to survive, they never took more than they needed. They understood that if they respected the buffalo and the land, the animals would continue to thrive and provide for future generations.

the significance of buffalo hunting in their culture

Buffalo hunting was more than just a way to get food for the Pawnee—it was a central part of their culture, shaping their way of life, their beliefs, and their connection to the land. The buffalo were considered sacred, and hunting them wasn't just a practical task, it was a deeply spiritual activity filled with meaning. Each hunt carried traditions and rituals, and the act of bringing down a buffalo involved cooperation, courage, and respect. The significance of buffalo hunting ran through every aspect of Pawnee life, from their daily survival to their spiritual practices.

When the Pawnee prepared for a buffalo hunt, it wasn't something they rushed into. The hunt had to be done right, and there was a great deal of planning involved. Pawnee men would spend time discussing strategies, deciding which herds to follow and how to approach them. The herds were constantly on the move across the Plains, and the Pawnee hunters had to track them, sometimes traveling for days just to find the right opportunity. The preparation for a hunt was part of what made the hunt itself so meaningful—it wasn't just about running after a herd, it was about thinking, planning, and working together to ensure success.

But there was more to it than strategy. Before setting out, the Pawnee often held spiritual ceremonies to ask for the blessing of the spirits and the buffalo. They believed that the buffalo had spirits of their own, and in order to have a successful hunt, they needed to approach the animals with respect and honor. These ceremonies were an important way for the Pawnee to acknowledge the significance of what they were about to do. They weren't hunting for sport or for fun—they were hunting to provide for their families and their village. The buffalo gave them life, and the Pawnee didn't take that lightly.

During the ceremonies, prayers would be offered, and the men would prepare themselves mentally and spiritually for the hunt. There might be songs and dances, all of which connected the hunters to their ancestors, the spirits, and the buffalo. The Pawnee believed that these rituals helped guide them in the hunt and ensured that they would return safely with the meat and materials they needed. Hunting wasn't just a physical challenge—it was also a test of a hunter's spiritual strength and connection to the natural world.

When the hunters finally set out, they relied on their knowledge of the land and the behavior of the buffalo. Buffalo herds were large, and the animals were strong and fast, which made them difficult to hunt. The Pawnee had to be patient and wait for the right moment to strike. They would often use the terrain to their advantage, driving the buffalo toward natural barriers like cliffs or rivers to make the hunt easier and safer. This required not just physical strength but also sharp observation and teamwork.

Teamwork was essential. The hunters depended on each other to corner the buffalo, to make sure that the herd didn't scatter, and to bring down the animals without injury to themselves. Each hunter had a specific role to play, and they trusted one another completely. This trust wasn't just about getting the buffalo—it was about their bond as members of the community. By working together, they could achieve more than any one person could on their own. This cooperation was deeply valued in Pawnee culture and reflected in the way they approached every hunt.

Once a buffalo was brought down, the real work began. The Pawnee didn't just celebrate the kill—they honored the buffalo for what it had given them. They believed that the spirit of the buffalo deserved respect, and they would often perform small rituals to thank the animal for its sacrifice. These rituals might include placing special objects near the buffalo's body or offering prayers of gratitude. This practice wasn't just about tradition—it was about maintaining a relationship with the natural world and acknowledging that the buffalo were not just resources but living beings that played a crucial role in the balance of life on the Plains.

After the buffalo was killed, the entire community came together to help process the animal. The hunters would bring the buffalo back to the village, where the women would take over, carefully butchering the animal and preparing the meat for the long months ahead. This communal effort was another way the hunt connected the Pawnee as a people. The success of the hunt wasn't just for the hunters themselves—it was for everyone in the village. The meat would feed families, the hides would provide clothing and shelter, and the bones would be made into tools and weapons. Every part of the buffalo was used, and in this way, the Pawnee showed their respect for the animal and the land.

Buffalo hunting was also an important way for Pawnee men to prove themselves. Young boys looked up to the older hunters and dreamed of the day when they could join a hunt. Hunting was seen as a rite of passage, and becoming a skilled hunter was one of the most important roles a young man could take on. Fathers and uncles would teach their sons the skills they needed—how to track the herds, how to use a bow and arrow, and how to stay calm and focused during the hunt. This wasn't just about becoming a good hunter—it was about becoming a strong, dependable member of the community.

For the Pawnee, buffalo hunting wasn't just about individual achievement—it was about contributing to the greater good. The best hunters were those who worked well with others, who respected the buffalo and the land, and who provided for their families without greed or waste. A successful hunter was celebrated not only for his skill but also for his character. He was someone who could be trusted, someone who valued cooperation and respect above all else. These values were what made buffalo hunting such an important part of Pawnee culture—it wasn't just about the hunt itself, but about the lessons it taught and the bonds it created.

Sarah Michaels

buffalo drives and preparation

A buffalo drive began long before the hunters even saw the herd. The Pawnee would first track the buffalo, often for days, following the signs that the herd left behind. They might find buffalo tracks in the soft earth, or spot tufts of fur caught on bushes, or see flattened grass where the buffalo had slept. Knowing where the herd was moving was important because the Pawnee needed to find the right location for the drive. Not every part of the Plains was suitable for such a hunt—there had to be natural barriers like cliffs or steep slopes that would help funnel the buffalo into a controlled area.

Once the herd was located, the real planning began. The Pawnee would gather to discuss the strategy for the drive. Everyone had a role to play. The best hunters would ride out on horseback, getting into position on the sides of the herd, while others would wait behind, ready to help direct the buffalo toward the chosen spot. The goal was to guide the buffalo without startling them. If the herd got spooked too early, they could scatter, making the hunt much more difficult. Timing was everything.

Buffalo drives were carefully coordinated. The hunters on horseback were essential because they could move quickly and keep pace with the herd. They didn't want to frighten the buffalo into a full-out stampede, but instead, they would guide the animals, using their speed and skill to keep the herd moving in the direction they wanted. Imagine being one of those hunters, riding alongside a thundering herd of buffalo, trying to stay calm and focused while keeping control of your horse and making sure the buffalo stayed on course. It took an incredible amount of courage and coordination.

One of the most important aspects of a successful buffalo drive was choosing the right location. The Pawnee knew their land well, and they used the natural features of the Plains to their advantage. Cliffs were one of the best tools for a buffalo drive. If the hunters could guide the buffalo toward a steep drop, the animals would be unable to stop in time, and some would fall over the edge. This might sound dangerous, and it was, but it was also an effective way to bring down several buffalo at once without having to chase them across the open plains. Once the buffalo had been driven to the cliff, the Pawnee could more easily finish the hunt.

But cliffs weren't the only way the Pawnee used the land during a buffalo drive. Sometimes, they would drive the buffalo into a narrow valley or toward a river, creating a natural barrier that made it harder for the herd to escape. The key was to create a situation where the buffalo had fewer options for running away, making it easier for the hunters to close in and take their shot.

The preparation for a buffalo drive wasn't just about strategy—it was also about making sure everyone knew their role and understood the importance of working together. Each hunter had a specific job, whether it was riding alongside the herd, helping to direct the buffalo, or waiting in a strategic position to make the final kill. There was no room for anyone to act on their own or try to show off. Buffalo hunting required patience and teamwork, and every decision was made with the well-being of the entire village in mind. A successful hunt meant enough food, clothing, and tools for everyone, so the stakes were high.

Before the drive began, there was often a sense of quiet focus among the hunters. This wasn't a time for jokes or distractions—it was a serious moment, and everyone knew how important it was to stay calm and prepared. The Pawnee believed that the spirits of the buffalo were watching, and they wanted to honor those spirits by hunting with respect and care. Many hunters would take a moment to say a prayer or ask for guidance from the spirits before the drive began. This spiritual connection to the buffalo was always present, and it reminded the Pawnee that they were not just taking an animal's life—they were receiving a gift from the earth.

When the buffalo drive finally began, the thundering sound of the herd's hooves could be heard from miles away. The ground shook as the buffalo moved across the plains, their large bodies creating dust clouds that rose up into the air. The hunters would ride alongside them, keeping the herd moving in the right direction, while those on foot or waiting in the distance prepared to join in. The excitement and energy of the drive were intense, but the Pawnee hunters remained focused, using all of their skill and knowledge to keep the hunt on track.

As the herd approached the chosen spot—whether it was a cliff, a river, or another natural barrier—the hunters would begin to close in. The goal was to bring the buffalo to a point where they couldn't escape, making it easier to bring down several animals at once. The Pawnee were incredibly skilled with their bows and arrows, and once the buffalo were in range, the hunters would begin to take their shots. The aim was always to make the kill as quick and humane as possible, honoring the buffalo's life and the gift it provided.

Once the buffalo were brought down, the real work began. The entire village would come together to help with the butchering and preparation of the animals. The women played a crucial role in this part of the process, using their knowledge and experience to carefully cut and preserve the meat. They would also prepare the hides, turning them into clothing, blankets, and other essential items for the village. Children often helped by carrying tools, gathering wood for fires, or learning from their parents how to process the buffalo. This was an important time for passing down knowledge and teaching the next generation how to honor the buffalo and their role in the community.

The buffalo drive wasn't just about getting food for the

village—it was a reminder of the Pawnee's connection to the land, the animals, and each other. It showed how important cooperation was, and how, by working together, they could achieve something far greater than any individual could on their own. The preparation and planning that went into a buffalo drive reflected the Pawnee's deep respect for the natural world and their understanding that survival depended on balance and harmony with the land.

4 / pawnee beliefs and traditions

THE PAWNEE DIDN'T JUST RELY on nature for food, shelter, and tools—they also looked to it for wisdom. Nature taught them when to plant their crops, when to hunt, and how to prepare for the changing seasons. The cycles of nature—spring, summer, fall, and winter—were like a rhythm that the Pawnee followed closely. They knew when to watch for signs in the plants and animals, like when the birds began migrating or when certain flowers bloomed. These signs told the Pawnee what was coming next, whether it was time to start planting or to prepare for the cold months ahead.

But the Pawnee didn't just learn from the world around them; they also looked up to the sky for guidance. The stars, moon, and sun weren't just distant lights to them. They were part of their spiritual world, and each one held special meaning. When the Pawnee looked up at the night sky, they saw stories written in the stars, stories that helped explain their world and their place in it. They believed the stars were connected to powerful spirits who watched over them and guided their actions.

One of the most important stars to the Pawnee was the Morning Star. This star, which appears just before dawn, had a special role in their religious beliefs. The Pawnee believed the Morning Star was a powerful god who brought life to the world. They honored it through ceremonies, thanking the Morning Star for protecting their crops and families. These ceremonies weren't just a way to ask for help—they were also a way for the Pawnee to show their gratitude for the blessings they received. By celebrating the stars, the Pawnee believed they were staying connected to the spirits that helped them.

The stars also helped the Pawnee plan their year. Just as farmers today look at calendars to know when to plant or harvest, the Pawnee used the stars to tell them when it was time for certain activities. The rising of certain constellations in the night sky signaled the start of the planting season, while others marked the time for the buffalo hunt. These constellations acted like guides, leading the Pawnee through the seasons and helping them know when to prepare for the future.

The Pawnee believed that the sky was divided into two worlds—the world of the Morning Star in the east, and the world of the Evening Star in the west. These two stars represented different but equally important parts of life. The Morning Star was seen as a male spirit, representing life, renewal, and the start of each day. The Evening Star, on the other hand, was viewed as female, symbolizing rest, the end of the day, and the mystery of the night. Together, these stars balanced each other, much like day and night or life and death. This balance was important to the Pawnee, who believed that harmony between opposites was key to a peaceful and successful life.

This idea of balance wasn't just seen in the stars. The Pawnee believed that all of nature worked in harmony, with each part playing an important role. The rivers, the animals, the plants, and even the winds were all connected. They saw the buffalo, for example, as more than just a source of food—they believed the buffalo were part of a larger system that kept the world in balance. By hunting only what they needed and using every part of the buffalo, the Pawnee believed they were helping maintain this balance. They knew that taking too much from the land could disrupt the natural order, which was something they wanted to avoid.

Their connection to nature was also reflected in the way they built their homes. The earth lodges the Pawnee lived in were made from the materials around them—wood, grass, and soil. These homes weren't just practical; they were also symbolic of the Pawnee's relationship with the earth. By building their homes from the land, the Pawnee believed they were becoming one with the earth, living in harmony with the world around them. The circular shape of the earth lodges also reflected the Pawnee's belief in cycles and balance, much like the cycles of the seasons or the movement of the stars.

At night, when the village was quiet, the stars would shine brightly above, and the Pawnee would look up, reminded that they were part of something much larger than themselves. The stars, with their constant, predictable movements, were a source of comfort and stability in a world that could sometimes be unpredictable. The Pawnee knew that the stars had been there long before them and would continue to shine long after they were gone. This gave them a sense of connection to the past and the future, knowing that their ancestors had looked up at the same stars, just as their children and grandchildren would in the future.

Children in Pawnee villages were taught to respect and understand the natural world from a very young age. They learned not just how to hunt or farm, but how to listen to the signs that nature provided. They were taught to watch the stars, to notice the changing colors of the leaves, and to pay attention to the behavior of the animals around them. Through these lessons, they learned how to live in balance with the earth, just as their ancestors had.

The stories told by the elders often centered on nature and the stars. These stories weren't just for entertainment

—they were ways to pass down important knowledge and values. A story about the stars might teach a lesson about patience or bravery, while a tale about the animals might show the importance of respect and gratitude. Through these stories, children learned that they were part of a much larger world, and that their actions had consequences for both the people and the land around them.

key ceremonies and spiritual beliefs

One of the most important ways the Pawnee expressed their spirituality was through ceremonies. These ceremonies were moments when the Pawnee came together as a community to honor the spirits, ask for guidance, or give thanks. Every ceremony had its own purpose, whether it was to celebrate the changing seasons, prepare for a hunt, or ensure a good harvest. Through these rituals, the Pawnee believed they could communicate with the spirits and maintain the balance between the physical and spiritual worlds.

One of the most important ceremonies for the Pawnee was the Morning Star Ceremony. The Morning Star held special significance for the Pawnee people, symbolizing life, renewal, and the power of creation. The Pawnee believed that the Morning Star was a male spirit who worked with the Evening Star, a female spirit, to bring balance to the world. This ceremony was usually held in the spring when the Pawnee were preparing to plant their crops, as it was seen as a way to ensure the earth would be fertile and provide the food they needed.

During the Morning Star Ceremony, the Pawnee would gather before dawn, waiting for the first light of the Morning Star to appear in the sky. This star, which rises just before the sun, was a symbol of hope and new beginnings. The ceremony would begin with prayers and songs, honoring the Morning Star and asking for its blessing. The Pawnee believed that by showing their respect, the Morning Star would ensure the success of their crops and protect their families throughout the year.

The Pawnee's ceremonies often involved more than just prayers. There were dances, songs, and offerings to the spirits, all of which had specific meanings. The dances were not just about movement—they were a way to communicate with the spirits, acting out stories and honoring the forces of nature that guided the Pawnee people. Drums and rattles would create rhythms that mimicked the heartbeat of the earth, while dancers moved in patterns that represented the cycles of life.

The women of the tribe played a crucial role in these ceremonies. While the men might be the ones leading the hunts or fighting in battles, the women were seen as keepers of life, nurturing the crops, the children, and the home. During ceremonies, women would often prepare offerings, such as corn or sacred herbs, to be given to the spirits. These offerings were placed on special altars, and the Pawnee believed that the spirits would accept them in exchange for their protection and blessings.

Another key ceremony in Pawnee culture was the Harvest Ceremony, which took place in the fall when the crops were ready to be gathered. This ceremony was a way of giving thanks to the earth for providing the food that would sustain the tribe through the winter. The Pawnee saw the earth as a living, breathing entity, and the Harvest Ceremony was a way of honoring that relationship. The tribe would come together, sharing food, stories, and songs, all while showing gratitude for the bounty they had received.

During the Harvest Ceremony, the Pawnee also celebrated the Corn Mother, a powerful spirit who was believed to have given the gift of corn to the people. Corn wasn't just a food source for the Pawnee—it was sacred, representing life and survival. The Corn Mother was honored with songs and prayers, and the first ears of corn were offered to her as a way of thanking her for the harvest. This act of gratitude was seen as essential for ensuring future harvests and maintaining the balance between the people and the earth.

In addition to these seasonal ceremonies, the Pawnee also had ceremonies that focused on specific life events. For example, when a child was born, there were rituals to welcome them into the world and ask for the spirits to protect them. The Pawnee believed that every child had a spirit guide, and part of the ceremony was to help the child connect with that guide. These ceremonies were filled with songs, blessings, and offerings, all designed to ensure the child would grow up healthy, strong, and connected to the spiritual world.

Marriage ceremonies were another important part of Pawnee life. When two people were joined in marriage, it wasn't just a union between them—it was a union between their families, their ancestors, and the spirits that guided them. The ceremony often took place under the open sky, with the stars as witnesses. The couple would exchange gifts, such as blankets or tools, and offer prayers to the spirits, asking for a long and prosperous life together. These ceremonies were a reminder that every aspect of life, from birth to marriage, was connected to the spiritual forces that shaped the world.

Death, too, was seen as part of the cycle of life. When a Pawnee person passed away, the tribe held special ceremonies to honor their spirit and help guide them to the afterlife. The Pawnee believed that after death, a person's spirit traveled to the stars, joining the ancestors who had come before them. The stars were thought to be the final resting place of the spirits, and by honoring them, the Pawnee ensured that their loved ones would find peace and continue to watch over the tribe from the sky.

The Pawnee's spiritual beliefs also influenced the way

they viewed the land and animals around them. They believed that everything in the natural world had a spirit, and that these spirits deserved respect. This respect was shown in the way they hunted, farmed, and used the resources of the earth. When they hunted buffalo, for example, they didn't just see the buffalo as a source of food —they saw it as a spiritual being that was offering its life to help the Pawnee survive. Because of this, the Pawnee made sure to use every part of the buffalo, from the meat to the bones to the hide, ensuring nothing was wasted.

the importance of corn

The story of corn, as the Pawnee understood it, began with the Corn Mother, a powerful spirit who, according to their beliefs, gave the gift of corn to the people. This wasn't just a story for the sake of storytelling—it was a reminder that the food they ate had a divine origin and that they were blessed to have it. The Corn Mother represented life, growth, and nourishment. Each time the Pawnee planted their fields, they were honoring her gift, and they made sure to show their gratitude through special ceremonies and rituals.

Before planting began each year, the Pawnee held a sacred ritual to prepare the land and honor the Corn Mother. This ceremony wasn't just about getting ready for the farming season—it was a way of asking for the Corn

Mother's blessing to ensure that the crops would grow strong and healthy. During this ceremony, the Pawnee would offer prayers and gifts, such as small portions of last year's corn or sacred herbs, placing them in the earth to show respect and gratitude. The ceremony was often led by the women of the tribe, as they were the ones primarily responsible for planting and tending the crops.

Planting corn wasn't just a task—it was a sacred duty. The Pawnee believed that the act of planting was a way to connect with the earth and the spirits that lived within it. The seeds weren't merely placed in the ground; they were carefully and respectfully planted, with the belief that each seed held the potential for life. As the women dug small holes in the earth, they would say prayers, asking the Corn Mother and the spirits of the land to watch over the crops. This deep connection to the land and the belief that the earth was alive with spirits made farming an act of both physical labor and spiritual devotion.

As the corn began to grow, the Pawnee would continue to care for it with the same sense of respect and reverence. Children would learn from their mothers how to tend the fields, how to weed around the young plants, and how to protect the crops from animals. But they weren't just learning farming techniques—they were learning how to live in balance with the earth. They were taught that the corn was a living being, one that needed care, respect, and attention.

Throughout the growing season, the Pawnee held smaller rituals and ceremonies to ensure the health of the corn. These ceremonies were often private, held within families or small groups, and were a way of checking in with the Corn Mother, thanking her for the growth they had seen so far and asking for her continued blessings. Each time they walked through the cornfields, the Pawnee were reminded of their connection to the land, the spirits, and their ancestors who had grown the same crops on the same land for generations.

Harvest time was one of the most important times of the year for the Pawnee, and it was marked with a grand ceremony to give thanks to the Corn Mother. The Harvest Ceremony wasn't just about gathering the crops—it was a time for the entire community to come together and celebrate the gift of life that the corn had provided. During this ceremony, the first ears of corn were treated as sacred objects, and they were offered back to the Corn Mother as a way of showing gratitude. The Pawnee believed that by giving back some of what the earth had provided, they were ensuring that the Corn Mother would continue to bless their crops in the future.

The Harvest Ceremony was filled with songs, dances, and prayers. The Pawnee would gather in a circle, holding hands, and move together in rhythmic patterns that represented the cycles of life and nature. The music, often created with drums and rattles, would rise up to the sky, a way of communicating with the spirits and the Corn Mother herself. These ceremonies weren't just a celebration of the physical harvest—they were a reminder that everything in life was a gift from the spirits, and that the Pawnee had a responsibility to honor and respect that gift.

Even after the corn was harvested and stored for the winter months, the Pawnee continued to show their gratitude. Every meal that included corn was seen as a reminder of the Corn Mother's gift, and families would often say prayers before eating, thanking her for the food that sustained them. Corn wasn't just something to fill their stomachs—it was a symbol of life, growth, and the continuing connection between the Pawnee and the spiritual world.

Corn also played a role in other ceremonies, not just those related to planting and harvest. During certain religious rituals, cornmeal was used as an offering, sprinkled on the ground or into the fire to ask for blessings or protection from the spirits. Cornmeal was also used in healing ceremonies, where the Pawnee would ask the spirits to help heal someone who was sick or injured. In these moments, corn was seen not just as food, but as a bridge between the physical and spiritual worlds, a way to connect with the forces that guided and protected the Pawnee people.

5 /
the pawnee warriors and protectors

IN PAWNEE SOCIETY, warriors were seen as protectors, leaders, and symbols of strength. They played a vital role in the community, defending their people from enemies, leading hunting parties, and upholding the values and traditions of the tribe. Being a warrior wasn't just about being brave in battle—it was about responsibility, honor, and dedication to the well-being of the entire tribe.

From a young age, Pawnee boys learned what it meant to be a warrior. It wasn't something they were born into, but something they earned through training, discipline, and courage. They would watch the older men of the village—their fathers, uncles, and brothers—preparing for hunts or returning from battles, and they would dream of the day when they, too, could prove themselves. The life of a warrior was full of challenges, but it was also one of the highest honors in Pawnee society.

The path to becoming a warrior started with learning essential skills. Boys were taught how to handle weapons like bows and arrows, spears, and knives, practicing their aim and learning the patience needed for a successful hunt or a fight. They would spend hours outside, honing their skills, sometimes competing with one another in friendly contests to see who could shoot the farthest or throw the most accurately. These weren't just games—they were lessons in focus, endurance, and precision, traits that every warrior needed to develop.

But being a warrior wasn't only about physical strength. Just as important was the mental and spiritual preparation that went into the role. Pawnee warriors were expected to be strong not only in body but also in mind and spirit. They needed to understand the importance of balance, respect, and wisdom. Elders would often teach the young men stories about great warriors of the past, sharing tales of bravery and sacrifice. These stories were more than entertainment; they were a way of passing down the values that every Pawnee warrior had to live by —honor, courage, and loyalty to their people.

One of the key responsibilities of a Pawnee warrior was to protect the tribe. Life on the Great Plains wasn't always peaceful. There were times when the Pawnee had to defend themselves from other tribes or outside threats.

Warriors were the first line of defense, and they took this role very seriously. But they weren't just fighters—they were also strategists. Pawnee warriors would gather together to plan their defense or organize raids, carefully thinking through every decision. They understood that rushing into battle without a plan could be dangerous, and they valued careful preparation.

A warrior's reputation was built not just on how many battles they fought but on how well they led and protected their people. A good warrior was one who could make smart decisions, lead with strength, and always act in the best interest of the tribe. It wasn't enough to be fearless in the face of danger—warriors were expected to be wise and thoughtful, always considering how their actions would affect the community.

Another important part of a warrior's life was participating in hunting expeditions. Hunting, particularly for buffalo, was a critical part of Pawnee survival, and the warriors often led these hunts. The skills they had developed in training—stealth, accuracy, and teamwork—were essential in these situations. The warriors would ride out ahead of the village, tracking the herds and deciding the best way to approach them. Just like in battle, hunting required careful planning and cooperation. The warriors had to work together, communicating silently through gestures or signals to ensure the hunt was successful.

The hunt was also a time when younger warriors could

prove themselves. A successful hunt wasn't just about bringing down a buffalo—it was about showing bravery, discipline, and respect for the animal and the land. Warriors who excelled in the hunt earned respect not only for their skill but for their ability to lead and protect the tribe's resources. The buffalo provided food, clothing, tools, and shelter for the tribe, and it was the warriors who helped ensure the village had what it needed to survive.

Spirituality was deeply woven into the life of a Pawnee warrior. Before going into battle or setting out on a hunt, many warriors would take time to pray, asking for guidance and protection from the spirits. They believed that the outcome of a battle or a hunt wasn't just determined by skill—it was also influenced by the will of the spirits. Warriors would sometimes carry special items with them, like feathers, stones, or sacred herbs, which they believed offered protection or brought them good fortune. These items were often given to them by their families or spiritual leaders, and they served as a reminder of their connection to the spiritual world.

Ceremonies also played an important role in a warrior's life. Before a major battle or hunt, the tribe would often gather to perform rituals that called upon the spirits for blessings. These ceremonies were a way of preparing the warriors, not just physically but emotionally and spiritually. The Pawnee believed that going into battle with the right mindset was just as important as having the right weapons. Through these rituals, warriors would focus their energy, clear their minds, and connect with the spirits, ensuring that they were fully prepared for whatever challenges lay ahead.

Being a warrior also came with the responsibility of passing down knowledge. Older warriors were expected to teach the younger generation, sharing their experiences and helping them develop the skills they would need. This wasn't just about training in weapons or tactics—it was about teaching the values that made a warrior truly honorable. A good warrior was someone who respected their elders, treated others with kindness, and always acted in the best interest of the tribe. These lessons were passed down through conversations, stories, and even through the example set by older warriors in their daily lives.

Warriors also had an important role in ceremonies of peace. While they were known for their strength in battle, warriors were also called upon to help negotiate peace between tribes. Their knowledge of strategy and their leadership skills made them valuable in these situations. They would travel to other tribes to discuss terms of peace, often bringing gifts or offerings to show their intentions. These peaceful negotiations were seen as just as important as battles, as they helped protect the tribe and ensure its survival without unnecessary conflict.

Sarah Michaels

how they defended their land and people

The Pawnee didn't fight for the sake of fighting. For them, defense wasn't about aggression or seeking out conflict; it was about ensuring the safety and survival of the tribe. Protecting their land meant protecting their food sources, their homes, and their way of life. If another tribe tried to take their hunting grounds or raid their villages, the Pawnee warriors were prepared to respond quickly and decisively.

One of the first things a warrior learned was the importance of knowing the land. The Great Plains stretched out in every direction, but the Pawnee knew every hill, river, and valley like the back of their hand. This knowledge was essential for defending their territory. A warrior could spot the best places to set up defenses, where an enemy might try to hide or how to use the land to their advantage in battle. By knowing their environment so well, the Pawnee could move swiftly and with confidence, whether they were outnumbered or facing unfamiliar foes.

When the threat of an attack arose, the Pawnee wouldn't just rush into battle. They believed in careful planning and strategy. Leaders among the warriors would gather to discuss the best course of action, often spending hours or even days observing their enemies before making a move. They would consider things like the size of the enemy force, the terrain, and the potential risks to their village. The Pawnee understood that a battle wasn't just about who had the most warriors—it was about who used their resources wisely and who had the best plan.

One of the key tactics the Pawnee used in defense was ambush. The open plains didn't offer many places to hide, but the Pawnee were clever in using what the land provided. They might set up an ambush near a riverbank, where the tall grasses could hide them from view, or use a rise in the land to conceal themselves from approaching enemies. By lying in wait, they could catch their enemies off guard, striking quickly and retreating before the other side had a chance to regroup. This tactic allowed them to defend their land with fewer warriors, using surprise as their biggest advantage.

The Pawnee were also skilled in using their surroundings to create natural defenses. For example, they might position themselves near a steep hill or a deep ravine, forcing their enemies into a difficult position where it would be harder to attack. In battle, the Pawnee warriors were fast and agile, moving quickly to avoid being trapped or overwhelmed. Their knowledge of the land gave them an edge, allowing them to control the battlefield and keep their enemies on the defensive.

But defense wasn't just about fighting. The Pawnee also used diplomacy as a way to protect their people. When tensions arose with neighboring tribes, the Pawnee leaders would sometimes send warriors as messengers, offering peace talks or negotiations before things escalated into violence. The warriors who went on these missions had to be both brave and wise, as they were entering enemy territory to try to prevent war. These peace missions weren't always successful, but they showed that the Pawnee valued their relationships with other tribes and understood that not every conflict needed to end in battle.

When battle was unavoidable, Pawnee warriors relied on their training and their connection to the spiritual world to guide them. Before going into battle, they would often participate in ceremonies to prepare themselves both mentally and spiritually. These ceremonies were a way of asking the spirits for protection and guidance, ensuring that the warriors were in the right frame of mind for what lay ahead. The Pawnee believed that by honoring the spirits, they would be granted the strength and courage needed to defend their people.

Warriors would sometimes carry sacred objects into battle—items given to them by spiritual leaders or passed down through their families. These objects, like feathers, stones, or small bundles of herbs, were believed to offer protection and to connect the warrior to the spiritual world. These items were more than just symbols—they were a reminder that the warriors were not fighting alone. The spirits of their ancestors and the natural world were with them, watching over them and helping them succeed.

The Pawnee also had a deep respect for their enemies.

While they fought fiercely to protect their land and people, they understood that their enemies were often in similar situations, defending their own homes and families. This respect was reflected in the way they treated captured enemies or those who surrendered. The Pawnee believed in showing mercy when it was possible, and they valued the idea of peace, even with those they had fought against. This balance between strength in battle and respect for others was a core part of their warrior culture.

After a battle, the warriors would return to their village, where they were greeted as heroes. But their victory wasn't celebrated with loud parties or grand displays—it was a time of reflection and gratitude. The Pawnee understood that war came with a cost, and even when they were successful in defending their land, they knew that loss and sacrifice were part of the experience. The tribe would come together to honor the warriors and to give thanks to the spirits for their protection.

notable pawnee leaders and warriors

One of the most well-known Pawnee leaders was Ruling His Son, a man remembered not only for his bravery but for his wisdom in navigating the challenges his people faced. Ruling His Son lived during a time when the Pawnee were facing increasing pressure from settlers moving westward, as well as from other tribes competing for land and resources. He understood that while it was important to defend their territory, the Pawnee also needed to find ways to coexist with these new forces, even when they posed a threat to the tribe's traditional way of life.

Ruling His Son's leadership was marked by his ability to balance the old ways with the new realities that his people were facing. He was a skilled warrior, but he was also a diplomat. He recognized that sometimes, strength came not from fighting but from negotiating peace. Ruling His Son often worked to find solutions that would prevent unnecessary conflict, whether that was through agreements with other tribes or discussions with U.S. government officials. He believed in protecting his people's land and culture, but he also understood the importance of building relationships that could ensure the Pawnee's long-term survival.

Another remarkable Pawnee leader was Knife Chief, known for his skill as a warrior and his dedication to the traditions of his people. Knife Chief was part of the Skidi Pawnee, one of the four main bands of the Pawnee Nation, and he played a key role in maintaining the strength and unity of his tribe. He was highly respected not only for his ability to lead warriors into battle but also for his commitment to spiritual practices that honored the Pawnee's connection to the earth and the spirits.

Knife Chief was particularly known for his efforts to

preserve the Pawnee's sacred rituals, even as outside influences threatened to disrupt their way of life. He believed that the spiritual ceremonies of the Pawnee were essential to the tribe's identity, and he worked to ensure that these traditions were passed down to future generations. Knife Chief often led these ceremonies himself, guiding his people in prayers and rituals that connected them to the spirits of the land, the sky, and their ancestors. His leadership was a reminder that strength wasn't just about physical power—it was about staying true to the values and beliefs that had sustained the Pawnee for generations.

In addition to these great leaders, the Pawnee had many warriors who became legends for their bravery and skill in battle. One such warrior was Petalesharo, who became famous not only for his abilities as a fighter but for an act of incredible courage and compassion. Petalesharo was the son of Knife Chief and grew up learning the ways of a warrior. He was known for his fierce dedication to protecting his people, but it was a moment of mercy that truly set him apart.

According to Pawnee tradition, the tribe sometimes held rituals that included the sacrifice of captives, a practice that was intended to honor the gods and ensure good fortune. However, when Petalesharo saw a young captive woman about to be sacrificed, he stepped in to save her. Risking his own life, he intervened and freed the woman, allowing her to return to her people unharmed. This act of bravery and kindness earned him great respect, not only among the Pawnee but among other tribes and even settlers who heard of his actions. Petalesharo's decision to save the woman showed that true courage wasn't always about fighting—it was about standing up for what was right, even when it went against tradition.

Another Pawnee warrior who left his mark was Chief Big Spotted Horse. Known for his strength and leadership in battle, Big Spotted Horse led his warriors with fierce determination. He fought to protect his people's land and way of life during a time when the pressures from settlers and other tribes were at their height. He was deeply committed to the Pawnee and took his responsibility as a leader seriously. Big Spotted Horse was not only a formidable warrior but also a man who inspired loyalty and respect from his people. His name became synonymous with bravery, and he was remembered for the way he defended his people against great odds.

Blue Hawk was another Pawnee warrior whose name became legendary. Blue Hawk was known for his incredible speed and agility in battle. His fellow warriors admired him for his ability to move swiftly across the plains, striking quickly and disappearing before his enemies even knew what had happened. He was often chosen to lead scouting missions because of his keen sense of observation and his ability to anticipate the movements of his enemies. Blue Hawk's leadership in these missions played a critical role in protecting the Pawnee from surprise attacks, and he became known for his intelligence and strategic thinking.

One of the last great Pawnee leaders was Chief Crooked Hand. He led his people during a time of significant upheaval, as the Pawnee were being forced onto reservations and their way of life was being dramatically altered. Despite the many challenges he faced, Crooked Hand remained committed to his people's survival. He worked tirelessly to ensure that the Pawnee could adapt to the changes while holding on to their culture and traditions. His leadership during these difficult times was a source of strength for his people, and he helped guide them through the transition into reservation life.

6 /
the changing world for the pawnee

AS THE PAWNEE people lived and thrived on the Great Plains, their lives were suddenly affected by the arrival of European settlers. At first, the settlers were unfamiliar faces, traveling across Pawnee lands with wagons, horses, and strange new tools. The encounters between the Pawnee and these newcomers were often cautious, with each side curious about the other. The settlers were part of larger movements of people coming from across the ocean, and as their numbers grew, the impact on the Pawnee became more significant.

When the settlers first arrived, the Pawnee observed them from a distance, unsure of their intentions. The settlers were different from the neighboring tribes the Pawnee had interacted with before. They spoke different languages, wore different clothing, and used tools and weapons the Pawnee had never seen. These early interactions were often neutral. Some settlers were just passing through, looking for new lands to farm or heading west to find gold or other opportunities. Others were traders, offering goods in exchange for items the Pawnee could provide, such as buffalo hides or food.

Trade between the Pawnee and the settlers introduced new goods to the tribe. Items like metal knives, pots, beads, and guns were exchanged for food, hides, and other resources the Pawnee had in abundance. For a time, this trade was mutually beneficial. The settlers needed the skills and knowledge of the Pawnee to survive on the unfamiliar Plains, and the Pawnee found value in some of the new tools and materials they received in return.

But as more and more settlers arrived, the dynamics began to shift. What had started as occasional encounters turned into a flood of people moving westward, building homes, farms, and towns on land that had once been the Pawnee's hunting grounds. The settlers were often looking for places to settle permanently, which put pressure on the Pawnee's way of life. As more land was taken for farming or divided into plots for towns, the Pawnee found themselves with less and less space to hunt and grow food. This shrinking land base caused tensions to rise.

The Pawnee also began to see changes in the buffalo herds. The settlers hunted buffalo for their own needs, but they often killed more than they could use, wasting large portions of the animals. The Pawnee, who relied on the buffalo for nearly every aspect of their lives, were deeply troubled by this. The buffalo were sacred to the Pawnee, and their disappearance threatened the very survival of the tribe. As the settlers' presence grew, the buffalo herds thinned, and the Pawnee were forced to travel farther and farther to find enough to sustain their people.

At the same time, diseases brought by the settlers started to spread among the Pawnee, causing devastating losses. These were illnesses that the Pawnee had never encountered before—smallpox, measles, and cholera. The tribe had no natural immunity to these diseases, and they spread quickly, taking a terrible toll on the population. Entire villages were affected, and the number of Pawnee people dwindled as the settlers continued to expand across the land.

The Pawnee were not passive in the face of these changes. They defended their land when necessary, but they also tried to adapt to the new realities they faced. Some Pawnee leaders sought to negotiate with the U.S. government, hoping to secure agreements that would protect their land and way of life. These negotiations were complicated, and the promises made by the government were not always kept. The Pawnee often found themselves agreeing to treaties that seemed to offer protection but ultimately led to more loss of land and resources.

One of the most significant interactions between the Pawnee and the settlers came with the construction of the railroads. As railroads were built across the Plains, they brought even more settlers, and the Pawnee were forced to make difficult decisions about how to respond. The railroads cut through traditional hunting grounds, disrupting not only the buffalo herds but also the movement of the Pawnee people. With the railroads came soldiers, who were tasked with protecting the settlers and railroad workers, leading to more clashes between the Pawnee and the growing settler population.

At the same time, there were moments of cooperation. Some Pawnee warriors worked as scouts for the U.S. Army, helping them navigate the unfamiliar Plains and providing valuable knowledge of the land. These warriors were highly respected for their skills and bravery, even as they struggled with the complex realities of their changing world. Working with the settlers was a way for some Pawnee to ensure their survival in a time of great uncertainty, but it was not without its challenges. Many felt the deep conflict between protecting their people and helping those who were, in many ways, contributing to the loss of their land.

The arrival of missionaries also had a profound impact on the Pawnee. Missionaries came to convert the Pawnee to Christianity and to encourage them to adopt European ways of life, such as farming in a more settled manner and living in permanent houses. Some Pawnee adopted these new practices, but others resisted, holding onto their traditions and spiritual beliefs. The tension between maintaining traditional Pawnee culture and adapting to the new ways introduced by the settlers was a constant struggle for the tribe.

As the years passed, the Pawnee were eventually forced onto reservations, far from their original homeland. This relocation was a painful process, as they were separated from the land they had lived on for generations. The reservation life was difficult, with limited resources and little opportunity to continue the hunting and farming practices they had relied on. The move to the reservation was a direct result of the interaction with settlers and the government policies that sought to open up the Plains for further settlement.

impact of westward expansion

For centuries, the Pawnee had lived in harmony with the land, relying on hunting, farming, and a deep connection to the natural world to sustain them. The Great Plains provided everything they needed—vast herds of buffalo, fertile land for crops like corn, and rivers that supplied fresh water. Their way of life was carefully balanced, with a strong sense of respect for the earth, the animals, and the spirits. However, as the United States began to expand westward in the 19th century, the Pawnee found themselves facing new challenges that they had never encountered before.

One of the first and most significant impacts of westward expansion was the loss of land. As settlers moved onto the Plains, they built farms, towns, and railroads, taking over the land that had been home to the Pawnee for generations. This wasn't just a matter of losing a place to live—it meant losing access to the resources that were essential to the Pawnee way of life. The buffalo herds, which had always roamed freely across the Plains, began to shrink as settlers hunted them for sport or to clear the land for farming. The Pawnee relied on the buffalo not only for food but for clothing, shelter, and tools. Without the buffalo, their survival became much more difficult.

The expansion of the railroads also had a profound effect on the Pawnee. The railroads cut through their traditional hunting grounds, and with the construction of rail lines came an influx of settlers and soldiers. These new arrivals often viewed the Pawnee as obstacles to their plans for farming and building new communities, which led to conflicts over land and resources. The railroads also made it easier for settlers to transport goods and people across the Plains, further increasing the pressure on the Pawnee to leave their lands and adapt to the new realities of life on the Plains.

The U.S. government played a major role in shaping the course of westward expansion, and its policies had a lasting impact on the Pawnee. Treaties were signed that promised to protect Pawnee land, but these agreements were often broken or ignored as the demand for land grew. The government wanted to move Native American tribes onto reservations, areas of land set aside for them to live on, which were often far from their original homelands. For the Pawnee, being moved onto a reservation meant being separated from the land they knew and loved. It also meant giving up their traditional way of life in exchange for a much more restricted existence.

The reservation system had its own set of challenges. The land designated for reservations was often not suitable for farming, and the Pawnee were expected to become more settled, abandoning their traditional nomadic ways of life in favor of farming as the settlers did. But the soil on many reservations was poor, and the Pawnee found it difficult to grow the crops they needed to feed their people. The buffalo, once so plentiful, were now almost entirely gone, and the Pawnee had to rely on government rations, which were often inadequate or late in arriving.

Another major change brought by westward expansion was the introduction of diseases that the Pawnee had never encountered before. Settlers brought with them illnesses like smallpox, measles, and cholera, which spread quickly among the Pawnee and other Native American tribes. These diseases devastated the population, killing many and weakening entire villages. The loss of so many people, especially elders who held important knowledge and traditions, was a deep blow to Pawnee society. As they struggled to survive both the loss of their land and the loss of their people, the Pawnee faced a future that looked very different from the life they had known.

Despite these challenges, the Pawnee tried to adapt to the changing world. Some Pawnee leaders believed that in order to survive, they would need to find ways to work with the U.S. government and the settlers. They signed treaties, hoping that by making agreements, they could protect at least some of their land and ensure the safety of their people. Others tried to hold onto their traditional ways as much as possible, resisting the pressure to adopt the customs of the settlers. This tension between adaptation and resistance was something many Native American tribes faced as westward expansion continued.

At the same time, there were moments of cooperation between the Pawnee and the U.S. government. Some Pawnee warriors worked as scouts for the U.S. Army, helping them navigate the unfamiliar Plains and providing valuable knowledge of the land. These warriors were highly respected for their skills, and many saw their work as a way to ensure the survival of their people in a rapidly changing world. By serving as scouts, the Pawnee were able to maintain some control over their lives, even as their traditional way of life was being altered.

However, cooperation didn't stop the erosion of the

Pawnee's land or way of life. The pressures of westward expansion continued to mount, and the Pawnee were eventually forced onto a reservation in what is now Oklahoma. The move was difficult and painful. Being separated from their homeland was a devastating loss, and life on the reservation was far from easy. The reservation system limited their freedom, and they were no longer able to live as they had on the Plains. The land they were given was often not good for farming, and without the buffalo, they had to rely on rations from the government to survive.

But even in the face of these immense challenges, the Pawnee did not give up. They found ways to preserve their culture, language, and traditions, even as they adapted to new ways of living. Elders continued to pass down stories and teachings to the younger generations, ensuring that the Pawnee's connection to their history and their identity remained strong. Ceremonies, songs, and spiritual practices that had been part of the Pawnee way of life for centuries were kept alive, even in the new environment of the reservation.

relocation

The Pawnee had lived for centuries in what is now Nebraska and Kansas, where the land was fertile, and the buffalo roamed freely. These lands weren't just where they lived—they were part of who they were. The fields where they planted corn, the rivers where they fished, and the Plains where they hunted were all woven into their cultural and spiritual identity. Leaving this land wasn't a choice for the Pawnee; it was something that was forced upon them by the government, which believed that relocating Native tribes was the best way to make room for settlers and ensure peace.

The Pawnee were moved to a reservation in what is now Oklahoma, far from the familiar territory they had known for so long. This journey wasn't easy. Traveling such a long distance, often on foot, with limited resources was exhausting, and many Pawnee people suffered along the way. Families packed up what they could carry, but they were leaving behind not only their homes but also their way of life. The buffalo herds, once so plentiful, were not part of the new landscape. The Pawnee had to rely on rations from the government instead of hunting for their food, and the land they were moved to was very different from what they were used to.

Once the Pawnee arrived on the reservation, they faced a host of new challenges. The land they were given was often unsuitable for farming, and many of the traditional ways the Pawnee had survived were no longer possible. The reservation system was designed to encourage Native people to adopt European-style farming and living, but the soil in Oklahoma was much poorer than what the Pawnee were used to in Nebraska. Growing the crops that had sustained them for generations, like corn, beans, and squash, was difficult. Without fertile land or access to buffalo, the Pawnee found it harder to feed their people, and they had to depend on government rations, which were often late or insufficient.

On the reservation, the Pawnee were also subjected to new rules and restrictions that limited their freedom. They could no longer move freely across the Plains as they had before, following the seasons and the buffalo herds. Instead, they were confined to a small area of land, unable to hunt, travel, or interact with other tribes as they once had. This loss of mobility was deeply felt, as the Pawnee had always been a people connected to the land and the natural rhythms of life on the Plains. The boundaries of the reservation created a sense of confinement that was foreign to the Pawnee way of life.

Life on the reservation also brought cultural challenges. The U.S. government, along with missionaries who came to the reservations, encouraged the Pawnee to abandon their traditional customs, language, and spiritual practices in favor of adopting European ways of life. Schools were established to teach Pawnee children English and to educate them in the customs of the settlers. In many cases, children were taken from their families and sent to boarding schools far away, where they were not allowed to speak their native language or practice their culture. This was part of a broader effort to assimilate Native American tribes into mainstream American society, but for the Pawnee, it was a painful process of losing their cultural identity.

The pressure to assimilate didn't just affect the children—it affected the entire community. The traditional ceremonies, dances, and spiritual practices that had been central to Pawnee life were discouraged or outright banned by government agents and missionaries. The Pawnee were expected to adopt Christianity and the lifestyle of the settlers, which created deep divisions within the community. Some Pawnee people tried to adapt to these changes, while others resisted, holding onto their traditions as a way to maintain their connection to their ancestors and their heritage.

The emotional toll of relocation was immense. For the Pawnee, the land they had left behind wasn't just a place to live—it was a part of their identity. The fields where their ancestors had planted corn, the rivers where they had fished, and the Plains where they had hunted buffalo were all sacred to them. Being forced to leave this land and live in a new, unfamiliar place created a deep sense of loss. Many Pawnee people mourned not only the loss of their homeland but also the way of life that had sustained them for generations.

Despite these challenges, the Pawnee showed remarkable resilience. They found ways to adapt to their new circumstances while still holding onto their culture and traditions. Elders played a crucial role in this, passing down stories, songs, and spiritual teachings to the younger generations. Even though they were far from their ancestral lands, the Pawnee continued to honor their connection to the earth and the spirits. Ceremonies were held in secret, and families kept the stories of their people alive, ensuring that the Pawnee's cultural identity remained strong.

Over time, some Pawnee families began to adapt to the new farming lifestyle that the government encouraged. They planted crops, built homes, and created new ways to provide for their families. But even as they adapted, they never forgot their roots. The land in Oklahoma became a new home, but the memory of the Great Plains and the old ways of life was always present in their hearts and minds.

7 /
pawnee today

IN MODERN TIMES, the Pawnee tribe has worked hard to rebuild their community. The Pawnee Nation of Oklahoma, as they are now known, is a federally recognized tribe with a government that continues to advocate for the well-being of its people. They have their own system of governance, complete with an elected tribal council and leadership that makes decisions for the tribe's future. This structure helps the Pawnee protect their interests, manage their land, and ensure that their cultural practices are preserved for future generations.

Education has become one of the most important tools the Pawnee use to secure their future. After years of facing policies that discouraged or even punished the use of their language and traditions, many Pawnee have reclaimed their cultural heritage. Language programs have been established to teach young people the Pawnee language, ensuring that it is not lost. There are also programs aimed at preserving Pawnee customs, music, and ceremonies. Elders play a critical role in this, sharing their knowledge with the younger generations and making sure that the teachings of the past continue to live on in modern times.

Health and wellness are also major concerns for the Pawnee. Like many Native American tribes, the Pawnee have faced health challenges brought on by poverty, lack of resources, and the historical trauma of relocation and cultural disruption. However, the Pawnee Nation has worked to improve healthcare for its members, establishing health clinics and programs that focus on both physical and mental health. This includes not only modern medical care but also traditional healing practices that have been passed down through generations. By blending modern healthcare with traditional approaches, the Pawnee are able to address the unique needs of their people in a holistic way.

One of the most significant efforts in modern times has been the preservation of Pawnee land and resources. While much of their ancestral land was taken during westward expansion, the Pawnee have continued to seek ways to reclaim and protect the land they still hold. In recent years, the tribe has been involved in efforts to protect sacred sites, negotiate for the return of ancestral lands, and manage their natural resources. Protecting the land is more than just a political or economic issue for the Pawnee—it is a spiritual responsibility. Their connection to the earth remains strong, and they see it as their duty to protect and care for it, just as their ancestors did.

Economic development has been another focus for the Pawnee Nation in modern times. Like many Native American tribes, the Pawnee have worked to build businesses and create opportunities for their people. Some tribes have turned to gaming, such as casinos, as a way to generate income, and the Pawnee have explored this as one option. However, they are also focused on a range of other economic activities, including agriculture, small businesses, and tourism. By creating new opportunities for work and income, the Pawnee Nation is helping its members build stable lives while remaining connected to their cultural heritage.

Cultural revitalization is at the heart of much of what the Pawnee are doing in modern times. After decades of pressure to assimilate into the dominant culture, many Pawnee are reconnecting with their traditions and spirituality. This has included a resurgence of interest in traditional ceremonies, dances, and songs. The Pawnee hold gatherings and powwows where they celebrate their culture, invite other tribes to join in, and share their history and traditions with the wider community. These events are not just celebrations—they are acts of cultural preservation, ensuring that the unique identity of the Pawnee people remains strong in the modern world.

The return of traditional ceremonies has been especially important. For years, many of these ceremonies were held in secret or not practiced at all due to government restrictions. Now, with a renewed sense of pride and freedom, the Pawnee are once again able to openly practice their spiritual beliefs. Ceremonies connected to the seasons, the earth, and the ancestors are regularly held, and young people are encouraged to participate, learning the importance of these rituals firsthand. This reconnection with spirituality has brought healing to many Pawnee, helping them navigate the challenges of the modern world while staying rooted in the values of their ancestors.

Another area where the Pawnee have made significant progress is in protecting their historical artifacts and cultural heritage. For many years, museums and collectors took items that were sacred to the Pawnee and displayed them without permission. Today, the Pawnee are working with museums and institutions to recover these artifacts and bring them back to their rightful place within the tribe. This effort is part of a broader movement among Native American tribes to reclaim their cultural heritage and ensure that it is treated with respect.

The Pawnee are also actively involved in advocacy for Native American rights on a national level. Tribal leaders work alongside other Native American nations to push for policies that protect their land, culture, and sovereignty. This includes efforts to ensure that treaties are honored, that Native voices are heard in political decisions, and that the unique needs of Native communities are addressed by the government. By standing together with other tribes, the Pawnee continue to fight for justice and recognition in a country that has often marginalized their voices.

For the Pawnee, modern times have brought both challenges and opportunities. While they continue to deal with the legacy of forced relocation, cultural suppression, and economic hardship, they have also found ways to reclaim their identity and build a brighter future. The Pawnee people are resilient, and they have proven time and again that they can adapt to changing circumstances while staying true to their roots.

Today, the Pawnee Nation is a thriving community. With a strong focus on education, cultural preservation, health, and economic development, the Pawnee are not only surviving but thriving in modern times. Their story is one of perseverance and renewal, showing that even in the face of great adversity, a community can find strength in its traditions and build a future that honors the past.

the tribe's efforts to preserve their culture and heritage

One of the most significant ways the Pawnee have preserved their culture is through language revitalization. Like many Native American tribes, the Pawnee saw their language slowly disappear as outside influences, particularly government policies and boarding schools, discouraged or outright banned the use of Native languages. At one time, fewer and fewer Pawnee people could speak their own language fluently, which posed a threat to their cultural survival. The tribe knew that language was a vital part of their identity, and without it, much of their heritage could be lost.

In response, the Pawnee Nation created programs to bring their language back to life. They established language classes for both children and adults, where fluent speakers teach others how to speak and understand Pawnee. Many of these efforts focus on children, ensuring that the youngest members of the tribe grow up with a strong connection to their language. Teachers use traditional stories, songs, and everyday conversation to help the children learn, making the language a part of their daily lives once again. For many Pawnee, this has been a source of great pride, as they see their language coming back to life, passed from generation to generation.

Another important part of the tribe's cultural preservation efforts is the revival of traditional ceremonies and spiritual practices. For a long time, these ceremonies were suppressed, with government policies banning Native spiritual practices and encouraging the adoption of Christianity. Many Pawnee ceremonies had to be practiced in secret, and some traditions nearly disappeared. However, in recent decades, the tribe has worked to bring these sacred rituals back into the open, recognizing their importance in maintaining the tribe's identity.

One of the most important ceremonies is the Pawnee Sun Dance, which holds deep spiritual significance for the tribe. The Sun Dance involves fasting, dancing, and prayer, and it is a time for the Pawnee to connect with the spirits, the earth, and their ancestors. After years of being forbidden, the Pawnee now practice the Sun Dance again, often in the summer when the earth is in full bloom. This ceremony, along with others, is a way for the Pawnee to honor their spiritual traditions and to teach younger members of the tribe about their cultural heritage. The tribe sees these ceremonies as more than just rituals—they are a way of keeping their connection to the past alive.

The preservation of Pawnee art and craftsmanship has also been an important part of the tribe's efforts to maintain their culture. Pawnee beadwork, pottery, and other traditional crafts have been passed down through the generations, with each piece reflecting the unique style and symbolism of the tribe. In modern times, these art forms are not only preserved but celebrated, with many Pawnee artists continuing to create works that showcase the beauty and meaning of their culture. Pawnee designs are often based on nature, such as stars, animals, and plants, and they tell stories about the tribe's history and beliefs.

The Pawnee have established art programs and workshops where young people can learn these traditional crafts, keeping the knowledge of how to create beadwork, pottery, and other items alive. Through these programs, younger members of the tribe learn not only the technical skills of crafting but also the deeper meanings behind each design. This artistic expression is a vital part of the Pawnee's cultural identity, and through it, they ensure that their stories and values continue to be shared.

Storytelling has always been a crucial part of Pawnee culture, and the tribe continues to emphasize its importance in preserving their history. Pawnee elders, who are considered the keepers of knowledge and tradition, play a central role in passing down the tribe's stories. These stories, often about the creation of the world, the role of animals and spirits, and the bravery of past warriors, teach important lessons about life, respect, and the connection between humans and nature.

In modern times, the Pawnee have embraced new ways to keep their stories alive. Some stories are now recorded in books, videos, and audio formats, making them more accessible to future generations. This is especially important as the tribe works to blend traditional oral storytelling with modern technology, ensuring that the rich heritage of the Pawnee is never forgotten. Whether told around a fire or shared through digital media, these stories remain a vital link between the past and the present.

The Pawnee are also working to preserve and protect

their sacred sites, many of which are located far from their current home in Oklahoma. These sites, which are scattered across their ancestral lands in Nebraska and Kansas, hold deep spiritual and historical significance for the tribe. The Pawnee see it as their responsibility to protect these places, ensuring that they are respected and cared for. They have worked with government agencies, historians, and other Native American tribes to protect these sites, making sure that they are not destroyed or disrespected by development or other activities.

Efforts to reclaim artifacts and cultural items taken from the Pawnee during the years of colonization and forced relocation are also a key part of the tribe's preservation work. Many sacred items, such as ceremonial objects, clothing, and tools, were taken from the Pawnee and displayed in museums or private collections. These items were often removed without permission, and for many years, the Pawnee had little control over them. However, in recent years, the tribe has worked to recover these items through negotiations with museums and collectors, bringing them back to their rightful place within the tribe. This effort is about more than just reclaiming objects—it's about restoring pieces of their culture that were taken away.

Education is a central part of the Pawnee Nation's strategy for preserving their culture. The tribe has worked to ensure that their history and heritage are taught not only within the Pawnee community but also in schools and universities. Through partnerships with educational institutions, the Pawnee have created programs that teach both Native and non-Native students about the tribe's history, culture, and contributions. This helps to build understanding and respect for the Pawnee, while also ensuring that their story is told accurately and with pride.

where the pawnee live today

Today, the Pawnee people live primarily in Oklahoma, where they were relocated during the 19th century. Despite the hardships of relocation and the loss of their ancestral lands in Nebraska and Kansas, the Pawnee have built a vibrant and strong community in their new home. Although their homeland is far behind them, the Pawnee Nation has continued to adapt, thrive, and preserve their cultural heritage, all while embracing the opportunities of modern life.

Many Pawnee live on or near the Pawnee Nation's headquarters in Pawnee, Oklahoma, a small town that serves as the heart of their community. This is where many tribal government offices are located, and it is the center for much of the tribe's cultural and social activities. While Pawnee people may live in various parts of Oklahoma and even across the United States, the town of Pawnee remains an important place where the tribe gathers for ceremonies, celebrations, and governance.

The Pawnee Nation of Oklahoma is a federally recognized tribe, which means they have a government-to-government relationship with the United States. The tribe is governed by an elected tribal council that oversees important decisions regarding land, health services, education, cultural preservation, and economic development. The council works closely with tribal members to ensure that the Pawnee Nation continues to grow and thrive. This leadership has played a key role in helping the Pawnee manage their resources and provide support to their community.

One way the Pawnee continue to thrive today is through economic development. Like many tribes, the Pawnee Nation has worked to create businesses and industries that benefit the tribe as a whole. This includes ventures in agriculture, where they grow crops and raise livestock, as well as tourism and small businesses. Some tribes have turned to gaming as a way to generate revenue, and the Pawnee are no exception. Casinos can provide a source of income that helps fund healthcare, education, and cultural programs for the tribe. However, the Pawnee have also focused on a range of other industries to diversify their economy and create jobs for their members.

Cultural preservation remains a top priority for the Pawnee people, and it's a key way they continue to thrive.

The Pawnee Nation has invested heavily in programs that ensure their language, traditions, and stories are passed on to future generations. Elders are essential in this effort, teaching children the Pawnee language and sharing stories about the tribe's history. The Pawnee language is a central part of their cultural identity, and many efforts are underway to make sure it is spoken and understood by younger generations. Language classes, immersion programs, and cultural camps help keep the Pawnee language alive and vibrant.

Beyond language, the Pawnee continue to hold sacred ceremonies and community gatherings that bring the tribe together. These events are not only spiritual in nature, but they are also important social gatherings where the Pawnee people can reconnect with one another, celebrate their shared heritage, and strengthen the bonds within the community. The annual Pawnee Homecoming, for instance, is one of the largest events for the tribe, where members return to Pawnee, Oklahoma, to participate in traditional dances, storytelling, and cultural activities. It's a time for celebration, reflection, and honoring the resilience of the Pawnee people.

Health and wellness are important priorities for the Pawnee Nation. The tribe has made strides in improving healthcare for its members, offering services through their health center located in Pawnee. This facility provides medical care, dental services, and mental health support, ensuring that the physical and emotional well-being of the tribe is looked after. The Pawnee people have faced historical trauma, and the health center takes a holistic approach to care by addressing both the physical and cultural aspects of health. This includes integrating traditional healing practices with modern medicine to create a well-rounded approach to healthcare.

Education is another area where the Pawnee Nation continues to thrive. The tribe offers scholarships and educational support to Pawnee students, helping them attend college or vocational schools. This commitment to education is about more than just academic success; it's about ensuring that young Pawnee people have the tools they need to succeed in the modern world while remaining connected to their roots. Many Pawnee youth are encouraged to learn not only traditional skills and stories but also how to navigate modern challenges like higher education, professional careers, and leadership roles.

At the same time, the Pawnee Nation has strengthened its connection to its historical homeland in Nebraska and Kansas. While the tribe is based in Oklahoma, efforts have been made to protect and preserve sacred sites in their original homelands. The Pawnee still feel a deep connection to these places, and by working with local governments, historians, and other organizations, they have been able to ensure that these sites are respected and remain accessible to the tribe for cultural and spiritual purposes.

The Pawnee also continue to play a role in broader Native American rights and advocacy movements. The tribe has been involved in efforts to protect Native sovereignty, ensure that treaties are honored, and advocate for the rights of Native peoples across the country. Through partnerships with other Native American tribes and organizations, the Pawnee are able to use their voice to influence national policies and decisions that impact Native communities.

While much has changed since the days when the Pawnee roamed the Great Plains, their spirit remains strong. Modern-day Pawnee people are doctors, teachers, artists, business leaders, and government officials. They live in both rural and urban settings, and while they embrace the conveniences and opportunities of modern life, they hold tight to their traditions, values, and identity. This blend of tradition and modernity is what makes the Pawnee Nation so resilient—adapting to new challenges while staying true to their history.

8 / fun facts about the pawnee

interesting trivia and lesser-known facts

DID you know that the Pawnee were among the best astronomers of the Native American tribes? They had an incredibly detailed understanding of the stars and used them for both spiritual and practical purposes. The Pawnee believed that the stars were home to powerful spirits, and they relied on the night sky to guide their decisions, from planting crops to planning hunts. One of the most important constellations to the Pawnee was what we now call the Pleiades, a cluster of stars they associated with the planting season. When these stars rose in the spring, it was time to start planting corn, one of their most sacred crops. The Pawnee also had specific ceremonies related to certain stars, believing that these celestial bodies held the keys to life's balance.

Another lesser-known fact about the Pawnee is their intricate social structure. The tribe was divided into four main bands, each with its own distinct identity: the Skidi, the Chaui, the Kitkehahki, and the Pitahauerat. These bands worked together but also had their own leaders, customs, and ceremonial practices. The Skidi, for instance, were known for their strong spiritual practices and their connection to the Morning Star, while the Chaui were regarded as the most politically powerful of the bands. Each band played a role in the larger tribe, and the Pawnee's ability to unite while maintaining their unique band identities was a key factor in their strength.

Here's a cool fact about Pawnee warfare: Pawnee warriors were famous for their strategy and skill in battle, but what made them especially effective was their use of stealth. They would often paint their faces and bodies with different colors and designs before going into battle. These designs weren't just for show—they had specific meanings. For example, red might symbolize strength and victory, while black could represent power and protection. Warriors believed that these paints gave them spiritual protection and made them more intimidating to their enemies. Some designs were passed down from one generation to the next, each with a story attached to it.

Speaking of warriors, did you know that the Pawnee had a fascinating tradition called the "Cut-Throat" ceremony? This wasn't as scary as it sounds—it was a way for young boys to prove their bravery and readiness to become men. In the ceremony, a boy would demonstrate his courage by taking on a physically challenging task, often related to hunting or protecting the village. Completing this task showed the tribe that he was ready to take on the responsibilities of a warrior. While this ritual may sound intense, it was an important part of Pawnee life and helped shape the next generation of leaders and protectors.

Moving from warriors to food, another interesting piece of Pawnee trivia involves their ingenious farming techniques. The Pawnee were some of the most successful farmers among the Plains tribes. Living on the Great Plains, they had to be resourceful in the way they planted and harvested crops. One technique they used was a form of companion planting, where they grew corn, beans, and squash together in the same fields. These three crops, often called the "Three Sisters," helped each other grow. The corn provided a tall stalk for the beans to climb, the beans added nitrogen to the soil, and the squash spread out across the ground, acting as a natural mulch to keep the soil moist. This farming method was both efficient and sustainable, allowing the Pawnee to harvest enough food to support their community even in challenging conditions.

Another fun fact is that the Pawnee had a unique relationship with the wolf. Wolves held a special place in

Pawnee culture and were often associated with bravery, intelligence, and loyalty. In fact, many Pawnee warriors identified with the spirit of the wolf and would incorporate wolf imagery into their clothing, weapons, and names. The wolf was seen as a guide and protector, and it's believed that Pawnee hunters would often observe wolves to learn better hunting techniques. The connection between the Pawnee and the wolf was so strong that it influenced many aspects of their culture, from their stories to their spiritual beliefs.

Here's something you might not expect: the Pawnee had an advanced knowledge of medicine and healing, using plants and herbs from the Great Plains to treat various illnesses and injuries. Pawnee healers were highly respected members of the tribe, and they carefully guarded the secrets of their remedies. For example, they used sage for purification, yucca for skin conditions, and wild cherry bark to relieve coughs. Some plants were considered so sacred that only certain individuals were allowed to collect and use them. Healing wasn't just about the physical body, though—it also involved the spirit. Many Pawnee healing ceremonies included prayers, songs, and offerings to the spirits, ensuring that the healing process was complete.

Another fascinating aspect of Pawnee life is their connection to bison, which went far beyond hunting for food. The Pawnee relied on bison for clothing, tools, and even their homes. But did you know that bison bones were used to make toys for children? Pawnee children would often play with small dolls and figures carved from bison bones. These toys weren't just for fun—they helped teach kids important skills and values, such as how to care for their families or how to prepare for hunts. Play was an important part of learning in Pawnee culture, and these toys connected children to the animals that were so essential to their way of life.

The Pawnee's history is also tied to some interesting interactions with European explorers and settlers. While many Native American tribes resisted the presence of settlers, the Pawnee often took a different approach. At times, they worked with explorers like Lewis and Clark, serving as scouts and guides on their journeys. The Pawnee knew the land better than anyone and could navigate the vast Plains with ease. Their knowledge of the terrain, weather, and wildlife was invaluable to the explorers, helping them survive in an unfamiliar and sometimes hostile environment. This cooperation didn't mean the Pawnee were always on friendly terms with settlers, but it shows how adaptable and resourceful they could be in navigating changing circumstances.

One last piece of Pawnee trivia involves their incredible oral history tradition. The Pawnee didn't write down their stories—they passed them down from generation to generation through storytelling. These stories weren't just for entertainment—they were a way of preserving the tribe's history, teaching moral lessons, and explaining the natural world. Each storyteller had the important job of keeping the tribe's knowledge alive. Today, many Pawnee people continue this tradition, sharing their stories with younger generations and ensuring that the wisdom of their ancestors lives on.

how the pawnee are remembered in american history

In the early days of American history, before settlers moved west, the Pawnee were one of the most powerful tribes on the Great Plains. Their homeland stretched across what is now Nebraska and Kansas, and they were known for their strong farming and hunting practices. They grew corn, beans, and squash, which made them skilled agriculturalists, and they followed the buffalo herds for hunting. The Pawnee way of life centered around the land, and their ability to live in harmony with the Plains made them an essential part of the ecosystem.

One of the ways the Pawnee are remembered in history is through their relationship with the buffalo. Like many Plains tribes, the Pawnee relied on the buffalo for nearly everything—food, clothing, shelter, and tools. But their connection to the buffalo wasn't just practical; it was also deeply spiritual. The Pawnee believed that the buffalo were a gift from the spirits, and they treated the animals with great respect. They used every part of the buffalo, wasting nothing, and honored the buffalo in their ceremonies and prayers. This sustainable way of life has become an important lesson in history, reminding us of the balance between humans and nature.

The Pawnee are also remembered for their advanced understanding of astronomy. Unlike many other tribes, the Pawnee had a detailed knowledge of the stars, which played a crucial role in their spiritual and practical lives. They used the stars to guide their planting and harvesting, and many of their ceremonies were based on the movements of constellations. The Morning Star and Evening Star were especially important in their culture, representing powerful spiritual forces. The Pawnee even built their villages in alignment with the stars, believing that the heavens reflected the order of life on earth. This deep connection to the stars is a unique aspect of Pawnee history and is often remembered when discussing the tribe's cultural contributions.

Throughout American history, the Pawnee have also been recognized for their complex relationships with other tribes and with settlers. Unlike some tribes that fiercely resisted European settlers, the Pawnee had a more nuanced approach. They were known for being both fierce warriors and skilled negotiators. When it came to defending their land and people, the Pawnee fought bravely against their enemies, including other

Plains tribes like the Sioux. However, they also formed alliances when it was in their best interest. For example, they often acted as scouts for the U.S. Army, helping guide settlers and soldiers through the Plains. These relationships weren't always easy, but the Pawnee found ways to navigate the rapidly changing world around them.

One notable moment in American history where the Pawnee played a key role was during the westward expansion. As settlers moved west and the United States sought to expand its territory, the Pawnee found themselves at the crossroads of change. They were one of the first tribes to sign treaties with the U.S. government, hoping to secure some protection for their lands and way of life. However, like many Native American tribes, the Pawnee soon discovered that these treaties were often broken, leading to the loss of their homelands and forced relocation to Oklahoma.

Despite this difficult chapter, the Pawnee are remembered for their resilience during the relocation period. Although they were removed from their ancestral lands and placed on a reservation far from their home, the Pawnee managed to rebuild their community. They adapted to new surroundings while maintaining their cultural traditions, language, and spiritual practices. Today, the Pawnee people are recognized for their ability to preserve their identity and heritage, even after being displaced from the land that had sustained them for generations.

Another way the Pawnee are remembered in American history is through their contributions to the country's military efforts. During the Indian Wars of the late 1800s, many Pawnee warriors served as scouts for the U.S. Army. They used their knowledge of the land to help guide soldiers and protect settlers from attacks. Pawnee scouts were known for their bravery and loyalty, and their contributions were highly valued by the military. The service of Pawnee scouts is an important part of the tribe's legacy, showcasing their adaptability and their willingness to work with the U.S. government, even during a time of great change.

The Pawnee are also remembered for their cultural revival in modern times. After years of cultural suppression, the tribe has worked hard to restore and celebrate their traditions. One important aspect of this revival is the preservation of the Pawnee language. For many years, the language was at risk of being lost, as government policies and boarding schools discouraged Native children from speaking their native tongue. However, through dedicated language programs, the Pawnee have brought their language back to life, teaching it to younger generations and ensuring it remains a central part of their identity.

Their efforts to reclaim sacred ceremonies are also a significant part of how the Pawnee are remembered today.

Ceremonies like the Sun Dance and the Harvest Dance, which had been suppressed for many years, have been revived and are now practiced openly. These ceremonies are not only spiritual events but also cultural celebrations, bringing together Pawnee people from across the country to honor their ancestors and maintain their connection to the earth.

The Pawnee's story is also preserved in museums and historical sites across the United States. The Pawnee Indian Village Museum in Kansas and the Pawnee Nation Museum in Oklahoma are two places where visitors can learn about the tribe's history, culture, and contributions to American life. These museums house artifacts, including tools, clothing, and ceremonial items, that provide a glimpse into the rich cultural heritage of the Pawnee. Through these exhibits, the Pawnee are remembered not just as a people of the past, but as a living and thriving community.

In addition to their historical legacy, the Pawnee have been honored through various commemorations in American culture. Towns, rivers, and even military units have been named after the Pawnee, serving as reminders of their influence on the history of the Plains and the United States. These names keep the memory of the Pawnee alive, acknowledging the important role they played in shaping the country's development.

glossary

Skidi (Skiridi)

The Skidi are one of the four main bands of the Pawnee tribe. The word "Skidi" often comes up when discussing Pawnee culture, especially their spiritual beliefs. The Skidi band had a deep connection to the Morning Star and Evening Star, two important figures in their spiritual world. The Skidi performed special ceremonies to honor these celestial beings, believing that the stars guided the fate of their people. While each Pawnee band had its own customs and leadership, the Skidi were particularly known for their strong spiritual traditions.

Morning Star

The Morning Star is one of the most sacred symbols in Pawnee spirituality. The Morning Star appears just before dawn and is associated with life, creation, and new beginnings. The Pawnee believed that the Morning Star was a powerful god who brought life to the world and helped the crops grow. They held ceremonies in honor of the Morning Star, particularly during planting season, to ensure the earth would be fertile and provide food for the tribe. The Pawnee's relationship with the Morning Star shows how closely connected their spiritual beliefs were to the natural world.

Earth Lodge

An earth lodge is a type of home the Pawnee used for centuries. Unlike the teepees you might picture when you think of Native American housing, the earth lodge was a sturdy, permanent structure made of wood, grass, and earth. These lodges were built to withstand the harsh weather of the Great Plains, providing shelter from extreme heat and cold. A typical Pawnee earth lodge was circular and large enough to house multiple families. The roof had a hole in the center to allow smoke from the cooking fire to escape. Earth lodges were more than just homes—they were places where Pawnee families gathered, cooked, told stories, and lived their daily lives.

Buffalo

Buffalo were central to the Pawnee way of life. The Plains tribes, including the Pawnee, depended on buffalo for food, clothing, tools, and even shelter. Every part of the buffalo was used in some way: the meat was eaten, the hides were turned into clothing or used for the covers of teepees, and the bones were made into tools and weapons. The buffalo weren't just a resource; they were respected as sacred animals, and hunting them was a spiritual act. The Pawnee believed that the buffalo were a gift from the spirits, and they treated them with great reverence.

Three Sisters

The term "Three Sisters" refers to the three main crops the Pawnee and other Native American tribes planted together: corn, beans, and squash. These crops were called the "Three Sisters" because they worked together to help each other grow. Corn provided a tall stalk for the beans to climb, beans added nutrients to the soil, and squash spread out on the ground, keeping the soil moist and preventing weeds from growing. This planting method was both efficient and sustainable, and it helped the Pawnee grow enough food to support their community.

Pawnee Scouts

During the westward expansion of the United States, Pawnee warriors sometimes worked as scouts for the U.S. Army. These Pawnee scouts used their knowledge of the Plains to guide soldiers through unfamiliar territory, helping them navigate the land and avoid danger. Pawnee scouts were known for their bravery and loyalty, and they

Glossary

played a key role in many military campaigns. While the Pawnee had a complicated relationship with the U.S. government, their work as scouts showed their adaptability and their efforts to find ways to survive in a rapidly changing world.

Reservation

A reservation is an area of land set aside by the U.S. government for Native American tribes. In the case of the Pawnee, they were forced to move from their homeland in Nebraska and Kansas to a reservation in Oklahoma. Life on the reservation was very different from their traditional way of life. The Pawnee had less land to farm and could no longer hunt buffalo as they had for generations. Despite these challenges, the Pawnee worked to build a new community on the reservation, holding onto their culture and traditions as much as possible.

Treaty

A treaty is an official agreement between two parties, usually countries or governments. Throughout American history, many treaties were signed between the U.S. government and Native American tribes, including the Pawnee. These treaties often promised that certain lands would be protected for the tribes in exchange for peace or the sale of other lands. However, many of these treaties were broken, and the promised protections were not always honored. The Pawnee, like many other tribes, lost much of their land despite the treaties they signed.

Sun Dance

The Sun Dance is one of the most important ceremonies in Pawnee spiritual life. It is a time for the tribe to come together to pray, dance, and give thanks to the spirits, especially the sun. The Sun Dance involves fasting, dancing, and offering prayers to ensure the tribe's continued well-being and connection to the natural world. The ceremony is not only spiritual but also a way to bring the community together, strengthening the bonds between Pawnee families and ensuring that their traditions are passed down to younger generations.

Sacred Bundle

A sacred bundle is a collection of objects that hold special spiritual significance for the Pawnee. These bundles might include items like feathers, bones, herbs, or other natural materials, and they were used in ceremonies to connect with the spirits. Each bundle had its own purpose and meaning, and they were often passed down through families for generations. The sacred bundles were believed to hold great power and were treated with the utmost respect. They played an important role in Pawnee spiritual practices, connecting the tribe to their ancestors and the spiritual forces that guided their lives.

Glossary

Powwow

A powwow is a gathering of Native American tribes to celebrate their cultures through music, dancing, storytelling, and other traditional practices. The Pawnee participate in powwows to honor their heritage and share their traditions with others. These events are not only a celebration of culture but also an opportunity for tribes to come together in friendship and unity. Powwows often include competitive dancing, drumming contests, and storytelling, and they serve as a way for the Pawnee to keep their culture alive in the modern world.

Pawnee Nation

Today, the Pawnee Nation refers to the modern-day government and community of the Pawnee people, based in Oklahoma. The Pawnee Nation governs itself through a tribal council and works to preserve the culture, language, and well-being of the tribe. The Pawnee Nation is involved in many aspects of life, from education to healthcare, ensuring that the tribe continues to thrive in the present while honoring their past.

Milton Keynes UK
Ingram Content Group UK Ltd.
UKHW020803121224
452111UK00025B/183